Wisdom
for a
High School
Grad

Wisdom
for a
High School
Grad

~

By Douglas Barry

RUNNING PRESS
PHILADELPHIA · LONDON

"Your college experience will broaden your mind, expand your horizons and significantly enhance your opportunities for success."

—JODY M. WAGNER,
Treasurer of Virginia

9   8   7   6   5   4   3   2   1
Digit on the right indicates the number of this printing

Library of Congress Control Number: 2004097156

ISBN 0-7624-2304-4

Cover design by Bill Jones
Cover image © Stockbyte/ PictureQuest
Interior design by Jan Greenberg
Edited by Greg Jones and Teresa Bonaddio
Typography: Garamond, Century Old Style, Bulldog, and DINEngschrift

Publisher's Note: All quotes and letters within are used by permission.

This book may be ordered by mail from the publisher.
Please include $2.50 for postage and handling.
But try your bookstore first!

Running Press Book Publishers
125 South Twenty-second Street
Philadelphia, Pennsylvania 19103-4399

Visit us on the web!
www.runningpress.com

To my family and friends

CONTENTS

Introduction

One day last summer (not long after graduating from high school), while I was surfing off the New Jersey coast, I suddenly became seized with fear and apprehension. No, I didn't hear the music from the movie *Jaws* playing in my head. The source of my anxiety was, in fact, the fact that I would be starting college in just a couple of months!

I had already chosen my school—Tulane University in New Orleans—and successfully completed all the required paperwork and registration responsibilities. And I thought that I had become mentally prepared for college throughout my senior year of high school. But on this beautiful summer day, without a care in the world, a bunch of serious questions hit me like a ton of bricks. (Luckily I didn't fall off my surfboard.)

What will college really be like?

What if the classes are too difficult to get good grades?

What if the major I chose turns out to be completely wrong for me?

What will become of my relationship with my girlfriend back home?

Will I lose touch with my friends?

Will it be hard to make new friends at college?

What if I can't hack it?

What am I supposed to get out of college?

My parents later told me all the things that good parents say to ease my worry. *You'll do great in school, just like you did in high school. You'll make plenty of friends, and your friends back home will always be there, even your girlfriend. Everything will be fine.*

Of course, I trusted my parents and was thankful for their concern and encouragement. But I needed to seek a second opinion. Since none of my friends knew any more than I did, I'd have to think outside the box to come up with a list of people who might help me with some solid advice and maybe even stories of their own. But where would I start?

It dawned on me that I could do the same thing I did when I decided, at age 13, to become a CEO, but didn't know how to go about it. Back then, I wrote letters to over 150 CEOs asking them what it was like and how to achieve that position. Most of them wrote back and provided incredible advice and sincere encouragement.

Well, why not write a letter and send it to a lot of successful people who had already completed college and could share their experiences with me? That's what I did, and the responses I've gotten have been extraordinary.

The letters I received from CEOs at age 13 were so good that my parents helped me turn it into a book, called *Wisdom for a Young CEO*. And now, I've decided to do the same with the letters I've gotten from these wonderful college grads and a couple of non-grads who were kind enough to take the time and write me with their often personal and always heartfelt advice on what to get out of college. In addition to these letters, I also went online and read commencement speeches given at universities in recent years by famous achievers in a variety of fields— their words are also included in this book, along with the name of the institution and the year of the speech.

The college experiences shared by these individuals, and the wide range of life success they've achieved afterward, has already inspired me to make the most out of my own college experience.

I hope it does the same for you.

Expectations

ANTICIPATE THE BEST AND WORST

ex.pec.ta.tions (noun):

prospects or hopes

—*American Heritage Dictionary*, **3rd Edition**

"I've always been a firm believer in testing the limits of your abilities, and I cannot think of a few better ways to challenge the mind and soul than an experience in higher education."

—ANTHONY ALEXANDER, PRESIDENT AND
CEO, FIRST ENERGY

I expect my college years to be the best times of my life. My parents expect me to get a world-class education, study hard, and come home as often as I can. I plan on coming home only when the school closes. You ask most college-bound students what they expect out of school, and they'll tell you that they want to get a good education and find a career. They tell their friends they expect a sweet party every weekend and lots of newfound freedom.

When I graduated high school I realized that my parents and none of my friends from home were coming with me to New Orleans, my brand new home. And New Orleans would have to be home, too, because I couldn't fly back to New Jersey every night after class and complain about how awful my day was. I wouldn't have any more home-cooked food or a room to call my own. I've eagerly awaited this moment of freedom for the past two years of high school, so I don't *expect* to be homesick. I expect to find friends fast, go to parties and, by the way, get some homework done every now and then. All the flaws and weaknesses I had in high school will very soon be erased as I make a new life for myself in a place where no one yet knows who I am.

The glaring contradiction is that every moment that brings me closer to college forces me to become more anxious about leaving all the most important and familiar aspects of home. Have I taken these things for granted for the past eighteen years? I miss home already, and I haven't even stepped foot onto campus, but I cannot bear to stay at home any longer. I am yearning to tear myself away from high school, from my family, from the pressures of being a confused teenager, but I am not ready to assume full responsibility and independence. The idea terrifies me of not fitting in at college just like it would "the new kid" transferring to a high school midway through the year. How am I going to handle being without any physical contact with my family, who I could always come home to and sulk in front of if a teacher gave me a bad grade?

Above all else, I feel like I have been going along all these eighteen years just to come to a point where none of the grades I've received, none of the relationships I've cultivated, and none of the things I've grown to love doing matter any more. I'm going to a place without all of these relationships, and for four years I am going to be making completely new ones. Is nothing I've done of any importance? Is this really what the rest of life is going to be like, creating things and then abandoning them?

I can still shake these fears off knowing that I am young, strong, and ready to face a new experience. I have spent these past eighteen years getting ready for this moment when I leave home for the first time.

August 4, 2004

Mr. Douglas Barry

Dear Mr. Barry:

Yes, go to college. It will indeed help you to figure out who you are. And it may well surprise you by being fun as well.

Good luck.

Best,

Bill Borders

"Things you thought were really smart two years ago may not seem as smart next year. But that's okay too. It's okay not to be absolutely sure what you want to do right now. Not everybody does know . . . you have the right to be whoever you want to be. And this, for me, is all that really matters."

—WHOOPI GOLDBERG, WELLESLEY COLLEGE, 2002

"So how do you know what is the right path to choose to get the result you desire? The answer is this. You won't. And accepting that greatly eases the anxiety of your life experiences."

—JON STEWART, William and Mary, 2004

"Invest in as much formal education as possible and continue learning throughout your lifetime."

—GEORGE W. BUSH, PRESIDENT OF THE UNITED STATES

"BUT MOSTLY, IT'S IMPORTANT FOR YOU TO UNDERSTAND THAT THIS IS
JUST A STEP. YOU'RE NOT GOING FORTH UNLESS YOU WALK."

—BILL COSBY, Wesleyan College, 1987

*"I believe many of the qualities that best prepared me for business
leadership were the qualities I learned as a student, particularly at
the United States Naval Academy. They included identifying the
right people for the task at hand, giving them not only the responsibility but also the authority and the resources to complete the
task, letting them know clearly they are responsible for results, and
supporting and encouraging them throughout their work."*

—CORBIN A. McNEILL, JR., CHAIRMAN,
PRESIDENT & CEO, PECO ENERGY

"A GOOD EDUCATION WILL DEVELOP YOUR CRITICAL FACULTY. A GOOD
TEACHER WILL HELP YOU SORT OUT THE GOOD FROM THE MEDIOCRE. BUT,
YOU WILL FIND OUT FOR YOURSELF WHAT IS GOOD."

—DANIEL TRAVANTI, Actor

Getting Prepared

"Many high school graduates feel the urge to take some time off and gain new experiences outside of a classroom environment. I certainly felt the same urge when I was younger. But I can say without hesitation that my decision to enter college—and eventually earn a law degree by taking evening courses at the University of Akron—have served me well, both from the standpoint of furthering my career and in leading a full and active life."

—ANTHONY ALEXANDER, PRESIDENT AND CHIEF EXECUTIVE OFFICER, FIRST ENERGY

My Advice to Students:
—*EDUCATION COUNTS*—

■ BILL GATES
CHAIRMAN, MICROSOFT

Hundreds of students send me e-mail each year asking for advice about education. They want to know what to study, or whether it's okay to drop out of college since that's what I did.

A smaller number of parents send messages, often poignant, seeking guidance for their son or daughter. "How can we steer our child toward success?" they ask.

My basic advice is simple and heartfelt: Get the best education you can. Take advantage of high school and college. Learn how to learn.

It's true that I dropped out of college to start Microsoft, but I was at Harvard for three years before dropping out—and I'd love to have the time to go back. As I've said before, nobody should drop out of college unless they believe they face the opportunity of a lifetime. And even then they should reconsider.

Kathy Cridland, a sixth-grade teacher in Ohio, wrote to say, "Several of my students claim that you never finished high school. Since you are a success, my students perceive that as a reason not to care much about getting a good education."

I finished high school!

The computer industry has lots of people who didn't finish college, but I'm not aware of any success stories that began with somebody dropping out of high school. I actually don't know any high school dropouts, let alone successful ones.

In my company's early years we had a bright part-time programmer who threatened to drop out of high school to work full-time. We told him no.

Quite a few of our people didn't finish college, but we discourage dropping out. Having a diploma certainly helps somebody who is looking to us for a job. College isn't the only place where information exists. You can learn in a library. But somebody handing you a book doesn't automatically foster learning. You want to learn with other people, ask questions, try out ideas and have a way to test your ability. It usually takes more than just a book.

Education should be broad, although it's fine to have deep interests, too.

In high school there were periods when I was highly focused on writing software, but for most of my high school years I had wide-ranging academic interests. My parents encouraged this, and I'm grateful that they did.

Although I attended a lot of different kinds of classes in college, I signed up for only one computer class the whole time. I read about all kinds of things.

One parent wrote to me that her 15-year-old son "lost himself in the hole of the computer." He got an A in Web site design, but other grades were sinking, she said.

The boy is making a mistake. High school and college offer you the best chance to learn broadly—math, history, various sciences—and to do projects with other kids that teach you first-hand about group dynamics. It's fine to take deep interest in computers, dance, language or any other discipline, but not if it jeopardizes breadth.

I think kids sometimes trap themselves into a narrow identity. I wonder if they've just decided, "Okay, I'm the person who's good at accounting."

A friend asks, "Hey, what have you been reading?"
"Well, I'm reading about accounting"

GEORGE BUSH

August 11, 2004

Dear Douglas,

Thank you for your letter of July 16.

As you look ahead to the challenges that life surely will present, keep in mind that there is much about which to be optimistic. The world is ripe with opportunity for those who work hard, get an education, and play by the rules.

Always do your best. Be a doer and not a critic. If you are fortunate enough to take something out of the system, put something back into it. Give life everything you've got -- don't look for the easy way out. Above all else, be yourself and have fun!

Good luck in all that lies ahead.

Sincerely,

G. Bush

"TOMORROW IS HERE TODAY, TOMORROW HAS ALREADY ARRIVED. IT IS
HERE ALL AROUND US SPROUTING UP LIKE PLANTS IN SPRINGTIME."

—LEONARD LAUDER, Connecticut College, 1989

"GOING TO COLLEGE IS NOT AN END IN ITSELF; IT IS MERELY A GUIDANCE IN FINDING WHAT YOU SHOULD BE DOING WITH YOUR LIFE."

—DR. MARK MALKOVICH, General Director, Newport Music Festival

"MAKE A LIST OF THE PEOPLE WHO DON'T BELIEVE IN YOU. . . . CALL THEM
TONIGHT, AND TELL THEM TO GO TO HELL! AND THEN YOU GATHER AROUND
YOU THE PEOPLE WHO DO BELIEVE IN YOU . . . AND THEN YOU MOVE ON
INTO THE FUTURE."

—RAY BRADBURY, Caltech, 2000

"The most important thing I learned in college was how to challenge with regularity, social injustices."

—CRYSTAL ARLENE KUYKENDALL, DOCTOR OF EDUCATION AND ATTORNEY-AT-LAW

"YOUR GREATEST POSSESSION IS ACTUALLY OPTIMISM."

—WYNTON MARSALIS, Musician, Connecticut College, 2001

"Do not take everything with a grain of salt—there is no every-thing—but take a lot of things with a grain of sale, and take even more . . . with a handful."

—LORRIE MOORE, ST. LAWRENCE UNIVERSITY, 2004

LOOKING BACK . . .

■ JOSEPH V. MELILLO
EXECUTIVE PRODUCER
BROOKLYN ACADEMY OF MUSIC

Q: *What was the most important thing you learned in college? Why?*
A: I wasn't prepared for adulthood. After finishing undergraduate work, I went to work and after a year; I went to grad school.

Q: *Did college help you to understand yourself? How?*
A: You bet! Life experiences.

Q: *Did the college experience help you become the person you are today?*
A: No. Graduate school.

Q: *Did you keep your high school friends?*
A: One

Embrace Diversity

"I enjoyed college not only for the academic learning, but for the intermingling with students of other races, religions, political beliefs, morals, ideas, backgrounds. In blending into a college society with other students you will most assuredly begin to understand yourself and who you are."

—JIM DAVIS, President/CEO, Paws, Inc.

Arthur Hiller

GOLDEN QUILL
8899 Beverly Boulevard, #702
Los Angeles, California 90048

August 11, 2004

Douglas Barry

Dear Douglas Barry:

You're having the same insecurities we all have when we go to college or make a change in life. I don't know if college will be the "best time of your life" but it will be *one* of the best times of your life.

I would say your only problem is a lack of faith in yourself. Looking at your "background", you are so ready for college and will learn and grow so much. Just believe in yourself. You can study and play and grow while keeping the friends and relationships you are geographically leaving. You are not emotionally leaving them. Some relationships will change, but some would change even if you didn't go away to college.

How many people can say they have written all you've written and done all you've already done at age eighteen? Just have faith in yourself and keep at it.

Best,

Arthur Hiller

"YOU ARE THE FORTUNATE ONES. YOU WERE BORN WITH BRAINS AND NATU-RAL ABILITY. YOU HAVE THE CAPACITY AND DRIVE TO EXCEL. YOU LIVE AT A TIME IN A COUNTRY WHERE YOU STILL HAVE FREEDOM."

—SAMUEL L. JACKSON, Vassar College, 2004

"My education prepared me for a career and for a life by helping me discover a wider world, people with different ways of thinking and what types of writing I was best suited for as a career."

—**BARBARA PETURA**, ASSOCIATE VICE PRESIDENT FOR UNIVERSITY RELATIONS, WASHINGTON STATE UNIVERSITY

"SO LISTEN, GENTLE MEN, GENTLE WOMEN, PULL YOUR HEARTS OUT OF YOUR ARMPITS, GET YOUR TUXEDOES OUT OF MOTHBALLS, PUT YOUR LONG RED DRESS ON, GIRLS, AND SNAP YOUR BREASTS INTO PLACE, AS WE GO SAILING ON TONGUES, LOVING, LIVING, LEARNING TO SPEAK WITHOUT A CRUTCH."

—SONIA SANCHEZ, Haverford College, 2004

"The important thing is to get your seat at the table. Name your dream, there's a place, people are pursuing it."

—CHRIS MATTHEWS, Hobart and William Smith Colleges, 2004

"IN HIGH SCHOOL THERE ARE NO OPTIONS; YOU GO TO CLASS. IN COLLEGE, PROFESSORS COULD CARE LESS WHETHER YOU SHOW UP OR NOT. COLLEGE ALLOWS YOUR CHOICES TO DICTATE YOUR CONSEQUENCES."

—KENNY ROGERS, Singer/Actor

"Don't become dissuaded or particularly thrown off course just because you are afraid. If you are afraid, all that indicates is that you are human and not insane."

—RUDY GIULIANI, Stoney Creek High School, Shanksville, Pennsylvania, 2002

LOOKING BACK . . .

■ REGIS PHILBIN
LIVE WITH REGIS AND KELLY

Q: *What was the most important thing you learned in college? Why?*

A: How little I knew til then.

Q: *Did college help you to understand yourself? How?*

A: The competition is tougher. You measure yourself against your classmates. They'll make you try harder to be better and you will.

Q: *Did the college experience help you become the person you are today?*

A: Absolutely. Those four years make a big difference. You'll expand your horizons a dozen ways. These are the maturing years to learn and absorb as much as you can about everything—especially if you are a writer.

Q: *Did you keep your high school friends?*

A: If you move away for your high school city, it's difficult to keep these friendships alive. It can be done—just harder.

Note: I'm impressed with your credentials so far.
You could be a great one. Good luck!

"The most important thing I learned in college was . . . how to get along with a wide range of people. Exchanging and exploring new ways of thinking."

—JOSH TAYLOR, ACTOR

"MAP OUT YOUR FUTURE—BUT DO IT IN PENCIL."

—JON BON JOVI, Monmouth University, 2001

"I grew into an adult during my college years as I developed a love of learning. I also began to realize what I did and did not want to do. College is the time to do that."

—JANET ROBINSON, EVP/COO, THE NEW YORK TIMES

"IN COLLEGE, I HAD THE OPPORTUNITY TO 'REMAKE' MYSELF. YOU ARE STARTING WITH A CLEAN SLATE AND ARE NOT HELD BACK BY YOUR HISTORY."

—BARRY VOGEL, Director of Administration, Johnson & Wales University

"I've always been a firm believer in testing the limits of your abilities—and I can think of few better ways to challenge the mind and soul than an experience in higher education."

—ANTHONY ALEXANDER, PRESIDENT AND CHIEF EXECUTIVE OFFICER, FIRST ENERGY

"THE COMPETITION IS TOUGHER. YOU MEASURE YOURSELF AGAINST YOUR CLASSMATES. THEY'LL MAKE YOU TRY HARDER TO BE BETTER AND YOU WILL."

—REGIS PHILBIN, *Live with Regis and Kelly*

Inspiring Opportunities

College gives a person a chance to explore many subjects and topics that might lead to a long-term career. Not to mention faculty inspiration that, again, might lead you to explore something you might not have explored otherwise."

—NANCY LITTLE, School Director,
National Academy School of Fine Arts

RACEWAY
AUTOMOTIVE GROUP

August 13, 2004

Douglas Barry

Dear Douglas,

I am in receipt of your letter requesting information regarding your upcoming opportunity to attend college. I find it fascinating that you have gone to such detail in finding the information you quest for.

In response to your letter, I regrettably did not attend college. Even though there are a multitude of reasons for such, I to this day regret the missed experiences that only college can afford you. At only thirty-five years old, it hasn't been too long ago that I was in your place pondering the same thoughts you have, itching to get into the business world and succeed in life. From then to now what I have learned is that you will have plenty of time for life's many experiences in work and relationships and take time now to enjoy what has been offered.

Upon completion, you will look back at many great new friendships that have developed and an increased knowledge base on life today and how to more accurately tackle your goals and dreams.

Good luck in school and keep me posted on your future developments.

Sincerely,

John Isgett
President
Raceway Automotive Group

"At that time, I had no idea how valuable the education would be for my whole business life."

—ULF BAUER, PRESIDENTIAL SPOKESMAN, GERMANY

"I learned . . . that everything counts. The smallest action has meaning because life is short."

—HARLEY JANE KOZAK, Novelist

"It's never easy to move away from a secure and familiar life at home, and sometimes it's difficult to keep in touch with old friends and acquaintances. But some of my closest relationships today were forged in the years after high school when I shared many rewarding experiences with my new friends in college."

—ANTHONY ALEXANDER, PRESIDENT AND CHIEF EXECUTIVE OFFICER, FIRST ENERGY

Larry Kane Consulting
A Division of Dynamic Images, Inc.

October 5, 2004

Mr. Douglas Barry

Dear Douglas,

My "college experience" is no doubt different from many of the accounts you have received. Mine is one of an opportunity lost that I will never be able to regain.

Although I am still involved in a 47-year career as a news anchor (37 years in Philadelphia), an author, news analyst, radio commentator and broadcast consultant, there are aspects of my early professional life that are missing. And it's my fault.

Back in the early sixties I walked away from a full four year college scholarship because of parallel developments in my life: I had begun working in radio at the age of fifteen. Therefore by the rime I attended college I was fully immersed in the broadcast business. College was a distraction to me. As my career flourished in the broadcasting world, I decided that on the job experience was more important. It was a fateful decision because I did guarantee a great career ahead.

When I dropped out of the University of Miami though, I made one mistake. Although my career was never affected by my lack of a degree, my life was. Although I became a TV anchor in the nation's fourth largest market at the age of 26, I never really had time to enjoy the fruits of college, mostly the social experience of learning about other people, the socialization skills that college provides and the one aspect of a college education that everyone forgets – the ability to mature as a well rounded individual, armed not just with good grades but a full understanding of the challenges of life. That, in addition to a wonderful learning experience, is what college should be about – gaining a full understanding of what you are as an individual.

Please don't misunderstand me. I think I've developed into a decent and giving person, which is the real measure of a person's life. But I also think that my failure to finish college made it much more difficult to cope with the frustrations and anxieties of early adulthood.

I regret not finishing what I started, and I hope that you and others will understand what a character building experience the college experience is.

Sincerely,

Larry Kane

"THROUGHOUT YOUR COLLEGE YEARS, YOU WILL UNDOUBTEDLY BE CHAL-
LENGED IN MANY RESPECTS—INTELLECTUALLY, MORALLY AND SOCIALLY.
TAKE THESE OPPORTUNITIES AS LEARNING EXPERIENCES. WITH EACH NEW
STRUGGLE COMES A NEW REALIZATION OF YOUR STRENGTHS."

—BOB DOLE, United States Senator

"Preparation for any career must begin with a solid base of good education. . . ."

—STEVE SANGER, Chief Executive Officer, General Mills

*"Instead of spending the time trying to find out who you really are
(a form of novel contemplation) focus on what you wish to become.
Decide on a goal and aim for it."*

—JOHN MORIATY, FORMER CHAIR OF OPERA
DEPARTMENT, NEW ENGLAND CONSERVATORY

"Get the best education you can and always ask questions of those around you if you want to succeed . . . always be inquisitive, always be competitive and always play to win. But you can only win if you know the rules and that is where the best education comes into play."

—CRAIG BARRETT, CEO, INTEL

"YES, GO TO COLLEGE. YES, STUDY HARD."

—HONORABLE JOHN PAUL STEVENS, Chief Justice, Supreme Court of the United States

"I learned that I didn't know nearly as much as I thought I did when I left high school."

—DONALD DEWEY, Dean of University's School of Natural and Social Sciences, California State University

Tackle Fear

"The first thing I want to say is don't be scared. With all the giddy excitement you feel—and that I feel with you as you graduate—my guess is you're also feeling a little uncertain today. You're suddenly grown . . . with your whole life in your hands. And you're being flung into a world that's running about as smoothly as a car with square wheels. I want you to know that it's OK to be uncertain. I'm uncertain, too. In a world like this, it's appropriate to be uncertain."

—ALAN ALDA, CONNECTICUT COLLEGE, 1980

Hopes for the Future

"How will you use this extraordinary opportunity? My hopes for you would be that you use this gift of education to expand your intellectual horizons, to engage in advanced citizenship, and to use every experience as a chance to learn more about yourself, those around you and the world. In essence, I want you to use these college years to hone and develop your intellectual, interpersonal and social skills so you can become extraordinary leaders."

—SCOTT S. COWEN, Tulane University, 2004

"Education is not simply about academic achievement. As spelled out in the Universal Declaration of Human Rights, it is about understanding, tolerating and friendship, which are the basis of peace in our world."

—ROGER ROSENBLATT,
BRIGHAM YOUNG UNIVERSITY, 1998

"The graduates never take the advice,
as I have learned from long experience.
The best advice I can give anybody about
going out into the world is this: Don't do it.
I have been out there. It is a mess."

—RUSSELL BAKER, CONNECTICUT COLLEGE, 1995

"First: compassion and competition can co-exist if you visualize your career as an obstacle course and not as a ladder."

—BARBARA J. KRUMSIEK, GEORGETOWN UNIVERSITY,
MCDONOUGH SCHOOL OF BUSINESS, 2002

"ABOVE ALL, BE THE HEROINE OF YOUR LIFE, NOT THE VICTIM. BECAUSE
YOU DON'T HAVE THE ALIBI MY CLASS HAD—THIS IS ONE OF THE GREAT
ACHIEVEMENTS AND MIXED BLESSINGS YOU INHERIT: UNLIKE US, YOU
CAN'T SAY NOBODY TOLD YOU THERE WERE OTHER OPTIONS. YOUR EDUCA-
TION IS A DRESS REHEARSAL FOR A LIFE THAT IS YOURS TO LEAD."

—NORA EPHRON, Wellesley College, 1996

"Swing hard. Don't let fear of failure cause you to hold anything back. Don't be afraid to try something new."

**—KAREN P. HUGHES, Counselor to the President of the United States,
Texas A&M University, 2002**

*"You have reached a stepping stone in your life, a place where you
can pause for a moment and enjoy the luxury of looking back on
the distance covered; but the thing about stepping stones is that you
always need to find another one up there ahead of you. Even if it is
panicky in midstream, there is no going back."*

—SEAMUS HEANEY, UNIVERSITY OF
NORTH CAROLINA, 1996

THE VICE PRESIDENT

WASHINGTON

August 20, 2004

Dear Douglas:

Thank you for your letter. I was pleased to know that you will be attending college, and I can appreciate your desire to prepare yourself for this new experience.

Last spring I had the honor of addressing the graduating class of Florida State University. The advice I gave to the graduates may be of interest to you, as you begin this exciting new chapter in your life.

Lynne joins me in wishing you all the best in your bright future.

Sincerely,

Dick Cheney

"IT MIGHT SEEM UNFAIR TO SAY IT NOW—AFTER YOU KNOCKED YOURSELF
OUT ON FINALS OR A THESIS—BUT THIS IS ABOUT MORE THAN GRADES.
NOT JUST WHAT YOU KNOW, BUT HOW YOU THINK. NOT JUST WHAT YOU
ARE, BUT WHO YOU ARE. NOT JUST YOUR BACKGROUND, BUT YOUR VALUE."

—GEORGE J. TENET, U.S. Director of Central Intelligence
Texas A&M University, 2004

"WHEN I WAS A YOUNG MUSICIAN, THE ONLY OPTION AVAILABLE TO PURSUE
SECONDARY EDUCATION IN MUSIC WAS TO ATTEND A CLASSICAL CONSERVA-
TORY. OBVIOUSLY, I DIDN'T CHOOSE THAT ROUTE, AND ALTHOUGH THE ONE I
ENDED UP TAKING HAS BEEN RATHER CIRCUITOUS, I AM TRULY PLEASED
THAT THE ROAD HAS TWISTED AND TURNED . . ."

BILLY JOEL, Berklee College of Music, 1993

Listen and Learn

"So as you go out there, to face a world that is much less secure and predictable than the one I faced upon graduation, keep an open mind, an open heart, an open soul. Value the opinions of others, particularly those who may disagree with you. Listen to them and learn. Be tolerant, compassionate, courageous. Remember: We are all in it together."

—KATHRYN S. FULLER, BROWN UNIVERSITY, 2004

Family

HANGING ON & LETTING GO
OF RELATIVES AND FRIENDS

fam.i.ly (noun):
a group of like things

—*American Heritage Dictionary,* **3rd Edition**

"As everyone sets out to make their way in life, you drift away, you lose some friends and gain others."

—ANTON DELFORNO, JUSTON RECORDS

I am especially connected to home because of the people that surround me. My friends have been eighteen years in the making; I've known some of these people almost as long as I've known my parents, and even longer than I've known my own sister. I've grown up with these friends, spent years confiding in them, trusting them, going through some of the most awkward years of life with them. In just a short amount of time I will have to abandon them for a totally different group of people and try to gain the same kinds of friendships in a few short months that I've spent years cultivating at home. What distresses me more is that all of my friends from home who are also leaving for school are going to be forced to do the same thing. Will they forget me when seas of new, diverse, and interesting faces surround them? Will I forget them?

I want to meet new people, but I'm terrified that the further I drift away from the idea of home, the quicker I will forget who I was in high school. I want those four years of my life to matter just as much as college is supposed to matter. I want to build on what I learned, keep it, and go off to college with all of the knowledge (and all of my relationships) still intact. More and more, college looks like a test to me; this could very well be the proving ground for my friendships. This will determine who my closest friends are and who from home means the most to me.

For the first time I will be living away from my support system, my family. They'd do the simplest things for me, and now that I am going away to school I will be forced to rely on myself for even the simple things. I have to study without dad's help and knowledge, make my bed, change my sheets, and wash my clothes (without begging mom to do it for me). Going away to school is a step in the direction towards independence. The toughest part of the entire prospect of leaving my family is that I could always count on them. They would help me no matter how much trouble I was in or take my side no matter how wrong I was. My mom told me once, "Doug, you could rob a bank and your father and I would probably say that the bank had too much money anyway and needed to be robbed."

College, the world I am on the fringe of, is something totally new and different. I am anxious, and a part of me does not want to leave the people who have become my support system. Will I keep in touch with everyone during and after school? Who is going to stick with me through these four years and who is going to fade away to a memory? These things I wonder as I admire the last fleeting sights of home: the neighbor mowing his lawn, the familiar childhood friend with whom I've lost touch waving and smiling.

"You can study and play and grow while keeping the friends and relationships you are geographically leaving. You are not emotionally leaving them. Some relationships will change, but some would change even if your didn't go away to college."

—ARTHUR HILLER, FEATURE FILM DIRECTOR

"MY BEST FRIENDS TODAY ARE STILL FRIENDS I MADE IN COLLEGE."

—CRYSTAL ARLENE KUYKENDALL, Doctor of Education and Attorney-at-Law

"College will certainly give you some of the best memories of your life, but I can tell you that this will be a time when you meet people who will become your friends for a lifetime, and will shape the course of your life. Nurture those friendships. Treasure them. Work on them. Your efforts at working on friendships will be rewarded many times over."

—BRIAN COLBATH, INSTRUCTOR, PROJECTS PLUS, INC.

LOOKING BACK . . .

■ BARRY VOGEL
DIRECTOR OF ADMINISTRATION,
JOHNSON AND WALES UNIVERSITY

Q: *What was the most important thing you learned in college? Why?*
A: Perseverance. And that often when you do not get what you want it is because there is an even better opportunity waiting for you.

Q: *Did college help you to understand yourself? How?*
A: Yes. I had to opportunity to "remake" myself. You are starting with a clean slate and are not held back by your history.

Q: *Did the college experience help you become the person you are today?*
A: Absolutely. It exposed me to the experiences and people that most influenced me personally and professionally.

Q: *Did you keep your high school friends?*
A: Unfortunately, no. I did for a while but we went in very different directions. I wish we had remained closer.

"ALL OF US HAVE A VOICE INSIDE THAT WILL SPEAK TO US IF WE LET IT. SOMETIMES IT'S EASY TO HEAR; SOMETIMES WE HAVE TO TURN DOWN THE VOLUME OF THE DISTRACTING NOISE AROUND US SO WE CAN LISTEN. THAT VOICE TELLS US IF WE ARE ON THE RIGHT TRACK. IT LETS US KNOW IF WE GIVE AS MUCH AS WE TAKE, IF WE WELCOME THE OPINIONS OF OTHERS, AND AT LEAST ACCEPT DIVERSITY EVEN IF WE ARE NOT ABLE TO EMBRACE IT."

—CHRISTOPHER REEVE, Ohio State University, 2003

"HAVE FAITH IN YOURSELF AND GET OUT THERE AND CONQUER THE WORLD IN YOUR OWN WAY, AT YOUR OWN TIME. THE HAPPIEST PEOPLE I KNOW ARE ALL LATE BLOOMERS. AND THE IMPORTANT THING AS YOU CONQUER THE WORLD IS TO TAKE CARE OF YOURSELF, TAKE CARE OF YOUR HEALTH, TAKE CARE OF EACH OTHER, RELAX, LAUGH, BREATHE. SO WHEN YOUR MOMENT COMES, YOU ARE FIT AND READY TO GO."

—SIGOURNEY WEAVER, Southern Connecticut State University, 2003

The Value of All Friendships

"I formed new friendships and have continued to do this as I have moved from location to location. I am not good at maintaining long-distance friendships. Although I continue to value these friends, we have gone our separate ways. I see some of these early friends occasionally—but infrequently. Relocating puts you in a new setting with new responsibilities at different stages of your life; the people that you work with and socialize with frequently tend to change as your home location changes. Life is a series of life changes—and perhaps 'the best is yet to be!'"

—JOYCE P. LOGAN, ASSOCIATE PROFESSOR, COLLEGE OF EDUCATION, UNIVERSITY OF KENTUCKY

LOOKING BACK . . .

■ JOYCE P. LOGAN
ASSOCIATE PROFESSOR
UNIVERSITY OF KENTUCKY

Q: *What was the most important thing you learned in college? Why?*
A: In addition to increasing content knowledge which provided a new foundation for graduate work, living independently away from home in a new environment helped me in the transition to adulthood and maturity for making decisions about my future.

Q: *Did college help you to understand yourself? How?*
A: Yes. Getting to know and interact with people from different locations and different states and making adjustments to a new environment helped me to form my own value system and broadened my understanding of others.

Q: *Did the college experience help you become the person you are today?*
A: Without the college experience, I could not have entered the professional world and had the variety of personal and professional experiences that have made me the person I am today.

Q: *Did you keep your high school friends?*
A: I formed new friendships and have continued to do that as I have moved from location to location. I am not good at maintaining long-distance friendship. Although I continue to value these friends, we have gone our separate ways. I see some of these early friends occasionally —but infrequently. Relocating puts you in a new setting with new respon-sibilities at different stages in your life; the people that you work with and socialize with frequently tend to change as your home location changes. Life is a series of life changes—and perhaps the "best is yet to be!"

Q: *If you didn't go to college, did you ever regret it? Why?*
A: I value education; not going to college places strict limitations on your work and your friends—and your potential growth and development as an individual.

76 South Main Street
Akron, Ohio 44308

Anthony J. Alexander
President and Chief Executive Officer

October 20, 2004

Douglas Barry

Dear Douglas:

Thank you for your thoughtful and direct letter. You did a good job of describing a fairly common dilemma facing young men and women, as they consider moving on to college.

Many high school graduates feel the urge to take some time off and gain new experiences outside of a classroom environment. I certainly felt the same urge when I was younger. But I can say without hesitation that my decision to enter college – and eventually earn a law degree by taking evening courses at The University of Akron – have served me well, both from the standpoint of furthering my career and in leading a full and active life.

It's never easy to move away from a secure and familiar life at home, and sometimes it's difficult to keep in touch with old friends and acquaintances. But some of my closest relationships today were forged in the years after high school, when I shared many rewarding experiences with my new friends in college, the Coast Guard and here at the electric company. And I continue to enjoy every opportunity to develop new relationships through my many contacts in the world of business.

None of this would be possible had I not taken that initial step after high school into college. I've always been a firm believer in testing the limits of your abilities – and I can think of few better ways to challenge the mind and soul than an experience in higher education.

Best of luck as you deal with this difficult decision. Just judging from your letter, I'm confident you'll make the right one.

Sincerely,

Tony Alexander

"I DID NOT KEEP MY HIGH SCHOOL FRIENDS FOR THE MOST PART. I DO HAVE ONE FRIEND WITH WHOM I'M STILL IN CONTACT OCCASIONALLY . . . OF COURSE WE DID HANG OUT TOGETHER IN COMMUNITY THEATRE SINCE 8TH GRADE, AND THOUGH WE DON'T TALK FOR MONTHS AT A TIME, WHEN WE DO COMMUNICATE, IT SEEMS AS THOUGH WE SPOKE YESTERDAY. . . ."

—LAURA EWALD, Professor, Murray State University

"Remember: Your name may be on the diploma, but you had lots of help getting it there."

—GEORGE J. TENET, U.S. Director of Central Intelligence,
Texas A & M University, 2004

"You're way too young to be thinking of . . . drifting away from high school friends. Life is a big book and you must go through many chapters. Just approach each new change as a challenge."

—DR. MARK MALKOVICH, GENERAL DIRECTOR,
NEWPORT MUSIC FESTIVAL

"Sing the melody line you hear in your own head, remember, you don't owe anybody any explanations, you don't owe your parents any explanations, you don't owe your professors any explanations."

—BONO, MUSICIAN, University of Pennsylvania, 2004

"We frequently act—and work—like fame and power and money and all the stuff we collect are our true loves. Yet really, what matters most are faith and the people that we love."

—KAREN P. HUGHES, FORMER COUNSELOR TO THE PRESIDENT OF THE UNITED STATES, TEXAS A & M UNIVERSITY, 2002

"UNFORTUNATELY, BECAUSE I ATTENDED AN OUT-OF-STATE COLLEGE, I LOST TOUCH WITH MANY OF MY HIGH SCHOOL FRIENDS. . . . IN SPEAKING WITH OTHERS, THIS IS NOT UNCOMMON."

—DR. ALBERT D. GRAHAM, JR., Director of Early Childhood & Federal/State Programs, Penns Grove-Carneys Point Regional School District

LOOKING BACK . . .

■ BASIL ZITELLI
M.D., CHILDREN'S HOSPITAL OF PITTSBURGH

Q: *What was the most important thing you learned in college? Why?*
A: Several things: not only content in my area of interest, but it broadened my education in areas I had never had the opportunity to explore before—music as well as sciences. Importantly, it also taught me self-discipline.

Q: *Did college help you to understand yourself? How?*
A: Absolutely, yes. Self-discipline; living in an "unconstrained" environment made me try to understand where I felt most comfortable being myself rather than trying to "fit in" with a crowd who did not share my values. It strengthened and challenged my own values.

Q: *Did the college experience help you become the person you are today?*
A: Yes—it began laying a foundation—but I am not the person today that I was then. I have continued to "evolve" intellectually, spiritually, emotionally, but college life laid the proper foundation for that growth.

Q: *Did you keep your high school friends?*
A: No

"Your success . . . may enrich you and your families and communities, but that is less important in the largest way than the fact that by practicing your skills and exercising your knowledge, you are also preserving them and perfecting them."

—ROBERT PINSKY, U.S. POET LAUREATE, STANFORD UNIVERSITY, 1999

"What matters in this life is more than winning for ourselves. What really matters is helping others win too. Even if it means slowing down and changing our course now and then."

—FRED MCFEELY (A.K.A. MISTER ROGERS), Dartmouth College, 2002

"THOUGH I RENEWED SOME FRIENDSHIPS AT A 50TH HIGH SCHOOL REUNION, A SMATTERING OF CORRESPONDENCE FOLLOWED, BUT SOON DIED. I AM AS MUCH TO BLAME FOR THIS AS OTHERS—PERHAPS MORE."

—DONALD DEWEY, Dean of University's School of Natural and Social Sciences, California State University

LOOKING BACK . . .

■ MARION BROOME
UNIVERSITY DEAN
INDIANA UNIVERSITY SCHOOL OF NURSING

Q: What was the most important thing you learned in college? Why?
A: You make life-long friends in college. Probably because you are often in the same major, away from your family and growing up. I too was hesitant from Jan-Sept before college (although very independent) and was homesick my first six weeks away.

Q: Did college help you to understand yourself? How?
A: We spent a lot of time talking about life, ourselves, our values. I took some great courses that opened my mind to new ideas. I had to problem solve things I never had to before (budget, time management, boys). I realized I was not quite the conformist I was in high school.

Q: Did the college experience help you become the person you are today?
A: It began the process. I actually went on later to get a masters and Ph.D. (in my 30's). These also expanded my self-awareness, my sense about 'people' and how 'book smart' I was. I think if I had had lots of doubts I would have stayed out and worked a year and then gone on. But I had had enough of working in high school.

Q: Did you keep your high school friends?
A: Only one, and we still get together when I go home. I did keep some friends the first year and enjoyed my 10th reunion but have always lived in another state which makes it harder.

Learn to Lean

"Believe in people. The further one goes in life, the more his/her accomplishments depend on other people. Create an environment in which everyone can contribute and where diversity in all its dimensions prospers."

—GEORGE FISHER, CHAIRMAN OF THE BOARD,
EASTMAN KODAK COMPANY

"Without courage you can't practice any other virtue consistently. You can't be consistently fair, consistently kind, consistently generous or merciful—and certainly consistently loving—without courage."

—MAYA ANGELOU, POET, Ithaca College, 1999

"I DID NOT KEEP ANY FRIENDS FROM HIGH SCHOOL. . . . I LOST TOUCH AFTER 5 – 10 YEARS."

—DOUGLAS MCCORKINDALE, Chairman, President and CEO, Gannett Company, Inc.

"Whether you are talking about education, career or service, you are talking about life . . . and life must have joy. It's supposed to be fun."

—BARBARA BUSH, Former First Lady, Wellesley College, 1990

LOOKING BACK . . .

■ **DR. ALBERT D. GRAHAM, JR.**
DIRECTOR OF EARLY CHILDHOOD AND
FEDERAL/STATE PROGRAMS, PENNS GROVE-
CARNEY'S POINT REGIONAL SCHOOL DISTRICT

Q: *What was the most important thing you learned in college? Why?*
A: Probably the most important thing I learned in college was to think for myself and not be afraid to express my own opinion. Prior to that, it was much easier to echo the viewpoint of my friends and not offer an opposing opinion for fear of offending someone.

College afforded me the opportunity to hear opposing points of view in an analytical and structured atmosphere. I learned one could disagree without being disagreeable.

Q: *Did college help you to understand yourself? How?*
A: Yes, college did help me develop a better understanding of myself by exposing me to a variety of learning experiences and an assortment of personalities and viewpoints.

Growing up in a basically rural community and graduating from a small high school contributed to my leading a rather sheltering life before entering college. Of course, as one grows older, matures and experiences life throughout the years it helps one to have an even better understanding of oneself, which is a never-ending, ongoing process.

Q: *Did the college experience help you become the person you are today?*
A: Absolutely!! I can honestly say that my college experiences did help me become the person I am today. I was fortunate to have professors who were not only competent in their fields but were caring, compassionate

individuals who strived to help you succeed academically and in life. Through their teachings and encouragement, I learned public services, even though not always monetarily rewarding, it was an honorable and noble calling.

Q: *Did you keep your high school friends?*
A: Unfortunately, because I attended an out-of-state college, I lost touch with many of my high school friends. Even though I returned to my hometown after graduating from college, most of my friends had moved and were starting careers and families in other states. In speaking with others, this is not an uncommon experience.

However, the silver lining to losing old high school friends is that new, long-lasting friendships are made while at college. I continually hear from my college classmates, many of whom are now lawyers, doctors, engineers, professors, businessmen, etc. Even though they are accomplished and successful individuals, they are still just Dave, Tom, Bert, John, Joan and Betty; all of whom would give you the shirt off their back if ever in need.

Q: *If you didn't go to college, did you ever regret it? Why?*
A: If I had never gone to college, I no doubt would have regretted it. College not only stimulated me intellectually but also provided me with the tools and skills necessary to appreciate life and all it has to offer. It certainly made me a more knowledgeable citizen and a more compassionate human being.

"IT'S NOT THE HONORS AND PRIZES AND THE FANCY OUTSIDES OF LIFE WHICH ULTIMATELY NOURISH OUR SOULS. IT'S THE KNOWING THAT WE CAN BE TRUSTED, THAT WE NEVER HAVE TO FEAR THE TRUTH, THAT THE BEDROCK OF OUR LIVES FROM WHICH WE MAKE OUR CHOICES IS VERY GOOD STUFF."

—FRED MCFEELY (A.K.A. MISTER ROGERS), Dartmouth College, 2002

"If you move away from your high school town, it's difficult to keep these [high school] friendships alive. It can be done—just harder."

—REGIS PHILBIN, *Live with Regis and Kelly*

"Most of us are able to succeed and rise in the world because someone helped out along the way, whether it was a memorable teacher or a boss who handed us a great opportunity, or the person who took a chance and gave us the first big break in our career. A grateful heart is an honest understanding of all that we have been given and all that is expected of us in return."

—DICK CHENEY, VICE PRESIDENT OF THE UNITED STATES, FLORIDA STATE UNIVERSITY, 2004

CRYSTAL ARLENE KUYKENDALL

Doctor of Education
Attorney-At-Law

August 10, 2004

Mr. Douglas Barry

Dear Douglas ,

I really enjoyed reading your letter of July 29, 2004. I took a few minutes to respond to your questionnaire. I have very fond memories of high school and college. I wish everyone could enjoy both experiences as much as I did. My best friends today are still friends I made in college.

Don't be afraid of "drifting" from your girlfriend. If she is your intended wife, nothing will keep you apart. I met my husband the summer after my high school graduation and we were married three years later.

I wish you much success in college and all of your future endeavors. If I can be of additional assistance, don't hesitate to contact me. You're certainly a young man with many incredible interests and a great future ahead of you. May God bless you bountifully and keep you in his care!

Sincerely,

Crystal Kuykendall

LOOKING BACK . . .

■ DONALD DEWEY
DEAN OF UNIVERSITY'S SCHOOL OF NATURAL
AND SOCIAL SCIENCES, CALIFORNIA STATE
UNIVERSITY

Q: *What was the most important thing you learned in college? Why?*
A: That I didn't know nearly as much as I thought I did when I left High School. To encounter new experiences and other people beyond the security of my community. Best time of my life? No way. I didn't feel that until I was in a doctoral program. But for me, high school wasn't that great either.

Q: *Did college help you to understand yourself? How?*
A: Yes, I entered the University thinking I was going to be an electrical engineer! While there I became a journalist. I left a position as city editor of a daily newspaper to take an advanced degree in history to make myself a better newsman. I eventually emerged with a doctorate, have been an administrator most of the remainder of my life and have had few regrets.

Q: *Did the college experience help you become the person you are today?*
A: I think the above answers this as well.

Q: *Did you keep your high school friends?*
A: No. Though I renewed some friendships at a high school reunion. A smattering of correspondences followed but soon died. I am as much to blame for this as others, perhaps more.

"Learning is an antidote because when we learn, no matter who we are and where we come from we still are marveling at the beauty of a sentence or cadence by Shakespeare, or an idea by Plato. Learning, therefore, is what brings people together. Continue to learn."

—ELIE WIESEL, DEPAUL UNIVERSITY, 1997

"The message of the myths is not the one that the gods would have us learn—that we should behave ourselves and know our place—but its exact opposite. It is that we must be guided by our natures."

—SALMAN RUSHDIE, Bard College, 1996

"HAVE SOME CHILDREN. CHILDREN ADD TEXTURE TO YOUR LIFE. THEY WILL SAVE YOU FROM TURNING INTO OLD FOGIES BEFORE YOU'RE MIDDLE-AGED. THEY WILL TEACH YOU HUMILITY."

—RUSSELL BAKER, Connecticut College, 1995

"I CAN PROMISE YOU THERE WILL BE PEOPLE IN YOUR LIFE WHO KEEP AN EYE ON YOU, WHO REWARD YOUR EFFORTS AND HELP BRING OUT YOUR STRENGTHS. SOMETIMES OTHERS KNOW BETTER THAN WE DO, JUST WHAT OUR GIFTS ARE AND HOW WE CAN BEST USE THEM. FOR ALL THE PLANS WE MAKE IN LIFE, SOMETIMES LIFE HAS OTHER PLANS FOR US."

—DICK CHENEY, Vice President of the United States

"Embrace discipline . . . discipline is not, as a lot of people think, some horrid exacting tortuous self flagellating activity—Discipline is just an expression of love. . . ."

—SUZAN-LORI PARKS, playwright, Mount Holyoke College, 2001

"SO, WHILE YOU ARE CONTINUING TO WALK DOWN THAT SOMETIMES-BUMPY ROAD OF LIFE, DEVELOP THE ART OF LAUGHTER AND JOY. KEEP YOUR BACKPACK OF TREASURES, THE WHOLE YOU, THE BEST YOU. THE 'YOU' THAT WON'T FEAR FAIL-URE, BECAUSE LESSONS LEARNED ARE THE ONLY WAY TO GROW."

—GOLDIE HAWN, American University, 2002

Wisdom of the World

"The two great requirements of the human animal, without which human community is corrupt or useless, namely, caring for the young ones and honoring the wisdom of the old ones, including the ways and wisdom of the dead. . . . If you come on a tribe that neglects its children or ignores its old ones, you know that some tremendous woe is about to extinguish that people's spirit."

—ROBERT PINSKY, STANFORD UNIVERSITY, 1999

"Nothing important, or meaningful, or beautiful, or interesting, or great ever came out of imitations. The thing that is really hard, and really amazing, is giving up on being perfect and beginning the work of becoming yourself. . . ."

—ANNA QUINDLEN, Mount Holyoke College, 1999

"The family is the cornerstone of our society. More than any other force it shapes the attitude, the hopes, the ambitions, and the values of the child. And when the family collapses it is the children that are usually damaged. When it happens on a massive scale the community itself is crippled."

—PRESIDENT LYNDON B. JOHNSON, HOWARD UNIVERSITY, 1965

"EACH OF US HAS THE POSSIBILITY OF BEING A COMPOSER, TO COMPOSE THE CLIMATE IN WHICH ONE LIVES . . . TO INDEED COMPOSE THE NEIGHBORHOOD, TO COMPOSE THE MELODY OF LIFE, TO COMPOSE THE RICHNESS OF IT."

—MAYA ANGELOU, Ithaca College, 1999

"A GOOD PERSON MEANS SOMEONE WITH A GOOD HEART, A SENSE OF COM-
MITMENT, A SENSE OF RESPONSIBILITY. EDUCATION AND THE WARM HEART,
THE COMPASSION HEART—IF YOU COMBINE THESE TWO, THEN YOUR EDU-
CATION, YOUR KNOWLEDGE, WILL BE CONSTRUCTIVE. THEN YOU ARE YOUR-
SELF THEN BECOMING A HAPPY PERSON."

—TENZIN GYATSO, HIS HOLINESS THE 14TH DALAI LAMA, Emory University, 1998

*"Think of your ancestors . . . among your ancestors have been
princes and slaves . . . if we seek among your tens of thousands of
ancestors, we will find not only slaves and royal personages, but the
product of love matches and rapes, people who died of starvation,
people who thrived, and across all those adventures and misadven-
tures, somehow the treasures have been passed on."*

—ROBERT PINSKY, STANFORD UNIVERSITY, 1999

The Source

"There are many ways that you, individually and collectively as a generation, will shape the institutions of business in the coming decades. Again, I would like to suggest that one of them is nothing less than, literally, to re-invent the corporation, and do it from the inside out, which means no matter where you begin your career, who you are matters."

—BARBARA J. KRUMSIEK,
GEORGETOWN UNIVERSITY, 2002

Horizons

SAILING TOWARDS THE UNKNOWN

ho.ri.zon (noun):
the range of one's knowledge, experience, or interest
—*American Heritage Dictionary*, **3rd Edition**

"Life is filled with serendipity—chance encounters, opportunities, and new people met. Stay open to seeing those opportunities for they may lead to careers, opportunities for service, friendships that you never dreamed of."

—BARBARA PETURA, ASSOCIATE VICE
PRESIDENT FOR UNIVERSITY RELATIONS,
WASHINGTON STATE UNIVERSITY

I'm looking at the vast Atlantic Ocean, which I know is teaming with all kinds of fish, mammals, sharks, and forests of seaweed. In the distance, past where I can see, there's an abyss filled with creatures people have never laid eyes on. *What kinds of creatures are gliding underneath my surfboard as I sit calmly atop this enormous body of water?*

When I think of college, that same feeling of the unknown creeps up on me. I only really know that when I leave I will be heading towards a new experience. Other than that, I am in the dark. Classes, schedules, and roommates may all change. I cannot be sure if I will study or party hard, if I will call home every day, every other day, or every other week. What if I don't call? I know I'll come home for certain breaks, see my family, see my friends. Will they be the same people after just a few short months of being without them nearly every day? It is the element of chance, fate perhaps, that leads me to believe that in not knowing what lies ahead of me I possess a unique sort of knowledge.

For all the preparation, the reading about my chosen school, the statistics about college, the academic credibility, and even the hard work in high school, the glaring, grinning fact is that I just don't know what awaits me. I can try to prepare, take all the advice my family and friends give me, and read endless volumes about the school and what other kids think about the school. The possibilities are utterly endless and to prepare and agonize over every little thing that could possibly happen is impossible. By preparing for school, I also don't want to over-prepare. I tell my mom not to show me what ranking Tulane University receives, what a certain article says about the school, or what her friend's daughter thought of the beautiful and lovely campus.

The unexpected is essentially what the college experience is all about. Will I be as happy at college as I am at home? One thing I do know is that most of the knowledge I will gain at school will come from the experience itself and not necessarily the classes.

The water is still cold because the sun has not been in the sky for more than two hours. I gaze at where the horizon and the Atlantic Ocean meet, touching each other, merging into an expansive, unseen world. I point my board uneasily towards the ocean as the new sun shimmers and wonder what my place is in this mysterious abyss.

August 31, 2004

Dear Douglas,

I am happy to answer your letter and to answer some of your questions. To begin, I looked forward with great anticipation to going to college from the time I was in middle school, and could hardly wait till that time came.

Certainly I enjoyed college, not only for the academic learning, but for the intermingling with students of other races, religions, political beliefs, morals, ideas, backgrounds....the list goes on. In blending into a college society with other students you will most assuredly begin to understand yourself and who you are. I believe you are well on your way to those goals at this time of your life.

You asked for advice to offer as I look back. When you go to college with a positive attitude, apply yourself, and take advantage of every opportunity to learn you will have accomplished not only personal satisfaction but will reach a higher level of maturity.

Is college better than high school? Certainly! Will it be the best time in your whole life? Who knows. It will be a great time. And for a while at least you will keep in touch with some of your high school friends...and probably your girl friend.

You love to surf. I love to play golf. These are amusements, not vocations. Relegate them to pleasant pastimes.

It seems that you have been extremely fortunate to have traveled extensively and have accomplished during your young writing career. My advice is to continue to write. Along with public speaking it is so necessary to whatever you do as your life progresses. Take advantage of everything that interests you that Tulane has to offer.

Best wishes,

Jim Davis

President/CEO
Paws Inc.

Paws Incorporated • 5440 E. County Road 450 N. • Albany, Indiana 47320-9728

"The events which really changed my life and made me the person I am today came long after I left college and arose from entirely unforeseeable events which challenged me in ways which college never did."

—COLIN PARRY, CHAIRMAN, CHILDREN FOR PEACE

"After some 14 years of professors at 6 public institutions in three states, I learned that information is not knowledge and knowledge only sometimes leads to wisdom. . . ."

—LAURA EWALD, PROFESSOR,
MURRAY STATE UNIVERSITY

"AS YOU MOVE THROUGH LIFE, LOOK AT EVERYTHING AS A LEARNING EXPERIENCE."

—KAREN MANTYLA, President of Quiet Power

Thomas R. Martin
Senior Vice President,
Director of Corporate Relations

ITT Industries, Inc.

4 West Red Oak Lane
White Plains, NY 10604

October 7, 2004

Douglas Barry

Dear Doug:

I am responding to your letter to Steve Loranger, our CEO. By way of introduction, I am responsible for Corporate Relations at ITT Industries, which includes Public Relations, Advertising, Government Relations, Employee Communications and Corporate Philanthropy. Normally letters like yours might get overlooked, but I chose to respond for a few reasons. First, I am the father of a college freshman, so I have recent experience with helping him think about many of the questions you pose in your letter. As an aside, he also has a girlfriend from high school and so far they are still together and still going strong. He has found it kind of a relief not having to be "in the hunt" every weekend like so many of his male classmates.

I also decided to respond because your letter was well-written. I was impressed, too, with your resume. I am asked to look at many resumes and yours was impressive, especially from a high school senior.

Like you, I was a writer in high school and college. I majored in English at Vanderbilt and certainly didn't know that I would end up as a business executive in Corporate Relations. But along the way I have always tried to put my writing first, and it has served me well. As to your other pursuits, they are impressive. I came to my love of the water later in life, but I am now an avid sailor.

To your questions, I would respond as follows. I think my most important lesson from college was the cause and effect relationship between hard work and honest reward. I was a mediocre student until mid-way through college when the light bulb went on and I realized that studying and learning could actually be fun. Thankfully that lesson has stayed with me over the years.

I'm not sure college helped me understand myself any better, but it did help me understand the world better, and to some degree my place in it. After college I worked and traveled in Europe for six months, and I think I learned more about myself in that time than in an equivalent year in college.

As to how the college experience helped me become the person I am today, I think it was a starting point. I think we are shaped by all of our life experiences, and the person I am today is not the same

as the person I will be tomorrow. George Bernard Shaw said that "we don't stop playing because we grow old, we grow old because we stop playing." My goal is to keep playing. When I was doing especially poorly in my first semester as a freshman, I considered dropping out and becoming a professional photographer. A wise person advised me to stay in school and take subjects that might eventually help me be a better photographer. It proved to be good advice as I survived the freshman year, got increasingly interested in the English major and finished with a respectable grade point average. I still like to take pictures, but I think I'm happier not having to do so to earn a living.

I have only a few friends from high school and college that I remain in close contact today. But I think the four years (or more) at college result in more transformation than any other four-year period of time in most people's lives. So I think it is often difficult to remain close to high school friends, particularly if life moves you to other places, both geographically and otherwise.

I don't know many people who chose not to go to college, but there are many famous dropouts, with Bill Gates being the most famous. I have met many wise people who did not go to college, and many knowledgeable college graduates who don't seem very wise. I think the best formula is to take the intelligence you are given, nurture it with as much knowledge as you can, and understand that more wisdom comes from life experiences than from good books or effective teachers.

I hope these answers are helpful in your research. The main advice I would offer is to stay curious, stay humble, stay healthy, and find as many ways as you can to help other people. When you are older and successful (as I strongly suspect you will be) and a high school student writes you a letter like the one you wrote to Steve, take time to answer it. I'm sure you will.

Good luck in your future pursuits. If you think about it, hang on to my address and send me a note to let me know how you're doing when you're at Tulane.

Sincerely,

Tom Martin

"Put blinders on to those things that conspire to hold you back, especially the ones in your own head. Guard your good mood. Listen to music every day, joke, and love and read more for fun, especially poetry."

—Meryl Streep, University of New Hampshire, 2003

"ONE OF THE THINGS PEOPLE ALWAYS SAY TO YOU IF YOU GET UPSET IS, DON'T TAKE IT PERSONALLY, BUT LISTEN HARD TO WHAT'S GOING ON AND, PLEASE, I BEG YOU, TAKE IT PERSONALLY."

—NORA EPHRON, Wellesley College, 1996

"The point is less what we choose, than that we have the power to make a choice."

—GLORIA STEINEM, Tufts University, 1987

Accept Sidetracks

"The road to success is sometimes defined by events that did not go as planned. My early interest was in politics, where I was very active in a political campaign, with the hope of continuing service after the re-election. When my candidate lost, I was forced to re-examine my career choices. I later found my niche in the business world."

—J. TERRENCE LAWIE, Chairman of the Board & CEO, MGM Mirage

"YOU WILL EVOLVE AND CHANGE— IT'S PART OF LIFE."

—WHOOPI GOLDBERG, Wellesley College, 2002

"The world is more malleable than you think and it's waiting for you to hammer it into shape."

—BONO, MUSICIAN, University of Pennsylvania, 2004

"I believe that getting the most you can out of your life experience is probably the best way to prepare to be a leader. . . . The best thing you can do is keep yourself open to a variety of experiences and not be afraid to make some mistakes."

—H. MCKINNELL, CHAIRMAN OF THE BOARD & CEO, PFIZER CORPORATION

August 13, 2004

Mr. Douglas Barry

Dear Mr. Barry:

Your letter reminded me of what my life was like during that time. As eager as I was for the adventure, I felt as though I was moving toward a cliff and was about to be pushed off. I was the bird being pushed out of the comfortable nest. Nobody is going to be able to offer you the comfort you are seeking because the experience is different for everyone.

Yes, college will be different from high school. Don't worry. It's good. It's part of becoming your own person. It all gets better.

You mention that you "cannot fathom the words 'career,' 'marriage,' or 'success' right now." Don't even try. I think many of us tend to try to figure out the rest of our lives before we know what we're going to do this afternoon. It's good to plan ahead, but don't feel as though you have to have a master plan. The trick is to take what comes along and make the best of it. I'm sure you will figure out that one for yourself.

I sincerely hope that college will <u>not</u> be "the best time" in your life, but will <u>prepare</u> you for the best days of your life yet to come. College will certainly give you some of the best memories of your life, but I can tell you that this will be a time when you meet people who will become your friends for a lifetime, and will shape the course of your life. Nurture those friendships. Treasure them. Work on them. Your efforts at working on friendships will be rewarded many times over.

None of these things did I do with particular grace. I learned as I went along and hope that I am still learning. From what you have written, I suspect that you are on the right track. Enjoy being happy. It is easier to be happy.

Sincerely,

Brian Colbath

Brian Colbath
Projects Plus, Inc

LOOKING BACK . . .

■ MAGGIE ROSWELL-RAYE
VOICE ACTRESS

Q: *What was the most important thing you learned in college? Why?*
A: A various background in numerous subjects as well as soup to nuts on acting.

Q: *Did college help you to understand yourself? How?*
A: Yes. Luckily, I had a passion. I pursued my major 24/7. My suggestion would be to find what it is that makes your heart sing, and major or minor in that.

Q: *Did the college experience help you become the person you are today?*
A: Absolutely. I believe had I not gone to 3 years of college, I would have been in an acting vacuum. Nothing to draw on. It's no surprise that half the young stars go back to college for life.

Q: *Did you keep your high school friends?*
A: Yes, but I went to an all girls Catholic High School. Most of my friends are high-end career/family babes—I am the token comic. (I wish I had minored in Business—I could have used it!)

Q: *If you didn't go to college, did you ever regret it? Why?*
A: I didn't finish. Trust me—if you have to expand your acting career into advertising, or teaching as a mentor, you have to have a college degree.

"Right or wrong, you have to step up
to the plate, even if you don't know
what you're doing."

—MEL GIBSON, LA Loyola Marymount University, 2003

"YOU HAVE THE SAME INSECURITIES WE ALL HAVE WHEN WE GO TO COL-
LEGE OR MAKE A CHANGE IN LIFE. I DON'T KNOW IF COLLEGE WILL BE 'THE
BEST TIME OF YOUR LIFE' BUT IT WILL BE ONE OF THE BEST TIMES OF
YOUR LIFE."

—ARTHUR HILLER, Feature Films Director

"MAY YOUR OWN DREAMS BE YOUR ONLY BOUNDARIES."

—VERNON E. JORDAN, JR., Writer

"Success is a lot like a bright, white tuxedo. You feel terrific when you get it, but then you're desperately afraid of getting it dirty, of spoiling it in any way."

—CONAN O'BRIEN, HARVARD UNIVERSITY, 2000

"GO TO COLLEGE. IT WILL INDEED HELP YOU TO FIGURE OUT WHO YOU ARE. AND, IT MAY SURPRISE YOU BY BEING FUN AS WELL."

—BILL BORDERS, News Editor, The New York Times

"I would not say that college is 'the best time of one's life.' But it is a time to prepare yourself for all of the rest of your life. What you choose vocationally could well far surpass the 'best times' of college. From your own description you have lots of God given talents, and are from a privileged background. 'To whom much is given, much is also required.'"

—BETTY J. LETZIG, CONSULTANT, GENERAL BOARD OF GLOBAL MINISTRIES, THE UNITED METHODIST CHURCH

Expand Your Horizons

"College, a unique experience, allows you the time and personal space to develop your intellect, expand your interests and generally shape your world view. By coming into contact with other young people from all over the nation and all over the globe, you will be better positioned to carve out your place in this complex internationally-linked world."

—JOHN F. KERRY, United States Senator

August 3, 2004

Dear Douglas,

Yours is such an interesting letter of July 27th that I decided to write you rather than fill in your five questions.

First of all, you are a big rascal. (And I love rascals!) You are not an "anxious teenage." Rather, you are a thoughtful, introspective and fun young man. I should like to know you.

Of course, you should go to college. If you have to ask a stranger, then, perhaps, you shouldn't go. But I can see that you are merely provocative. You must have given your dear parents a real run for their money! College will not necessarily be "the best time of your (my) life." It is just another step toward maturity and personal fulfillment. God has given many gifts, Douglas: you're smart intellectually, you must have a good body with that weight lifting, you are both artistic and athletic; both extrovertically inquiring and introvertively pensive. Those are good combinations.

You're way too young to be thinking of marriage or drifting away from your girlfriend. Life is a big book, and you must go through many chapters. Just approach each new challenge as a challenge. But most of all develop your spiritual life.

Like the Greeks of old, there are three important parts to our life: the physical, the intellectual and the spiritual. They are somewhat like a three-legged stool. The trick is to keep all three legs in balance. Develop each simul-

taneously. Then you will see that no matter what you do in life, you will be a success if you do what God intends of you. In the end it is not how many doctorates you have (I happen to have three) or how much money or fame you acquire, but rather that you are doing what God intends of you. Part of doing His will is doing what you love the best. If it's writing, then pursue that with avengeance. But going to college is not an end in itself; it is merely a guidance in finding what you should be doing with your life. When you are multi-talented (as I was myself at your age), then the decisions become more difficult. I became a chemist merely because I learned that that was the highest paid profession at that time in the late '40s. But at Columbia in New York City I did graduate work in literature and languages and studied with professors who were interesting and accomplished, such as: Margaret Mead in anthropology, Mark Van Doren in literature, Padriac Colum, the great Irish poet, himself a student of Yeats and godfather to James Joyce's son. He was mentioned by Joyce in "Ulysses." So imagine studying "Ulysses" with someone who is mentioned in it. I had a drama class with Gertrude Lawrence, who skipped her Broadway Wednesday matinee in the "King and I" to teach a class at Columbia. I went through Columbia with joy.

That is what you must do, Douglas. Tulane is a wonderful university. You will experience a great feast: taste of everything it has to offer. Continue your very wide pendulum swing of interests. You will be given direction as time passes. Just be open to any great possibility.

Aren't you blessed by God already. You have "excellent" health and parents who are obviously exceptional. You are a clever young man; use it for the good of others, not yourself. There is a bit of a con-man in you. You know exactly how to impress others and to get what you want for yourself. But don't do that. Rather,

look inwardly. The kingdom of God is within us. You needn't look all about you. I say to you what the chaplin at Columbia once told me: "Malkovich, you really have an inferiority complex; the trouble is that you never find anyone inferior to you!" So, I say the same to you, "Barry, ..." However, I am glad that I have that personality. It keeps me bumble. I always give the other person all the credit, though often I wind up picking up the pieces. I think that you are quite the same. But just keep on going.

Professor Colum lived to be in his mid-nineties. He was interviewed at a nursing home by the New York Times. The reporter asked him the secret of longevity, success, and happiness. It became a front-page article. And that dear Padriac said with his wonderfully Irish brogue which I can still hear: "Aye, just muddle through." So I leave with those same words. You'll know what that truly means when you get a little older....

Sincerely,

Mark P. Malkovich, III
General Director,
Newport Music Festival

"IS COLLEGE GOING TO BE 'THE BEST TIME OF YOUR LIFE'? THE ANSWER IS UNDOUBTEDLY 'YES' . . . COMPARED TO THE LIFE YOU HAVE HAD UP TO THIS TIME, BUT PROBABLY NOT WHEN COMPARED TO THE LIFE YOU WILL HAVE AFTER COLLEGE."

—COLIN PARRY, Chairman, Children for Peace

"LET THE WILD REVOLUTION START."

—Maurice Sendak, Goucher College, 2004

"THE BIGGEST MISTAKE YOU CAN MAKE IS TO BE COMPLACENT AND THINK THAT YOU HAVE LOTS OF EXTRA TIME ON YOU HAND. . . . THERE'S SO MUCH TO DO THAT YOU CAN'T POSSIBLY LET ONE SECOND SLIP BY THAT'S NOT FILLED TO THE BRIM."

—DR. RUTH WESTHEIMER, Trinity College, 2004

"Be prepared to work much harder than
you are now expecting. . . .
College is not high school!"

—**BARBARA PETURA, Associate Vice President for University Relations,Washington
State University**

"I SUPPOSE I BECAME SUCCESSFUL BY A COMBINATION OF DUMB LUCK,
LOW CUNNING, AND RISK-TAKING BORN OUT OF CURIOSITY. I STILL OPERATE
IN THE SAME WAY. . . . THERE'S ALWAYS SOMETHING MORE TO LEARN."

—STING, Berklee College of Music, 1994

"College did me a world of good."

—**SAM WATERSTON, Actor**

August 28, 2004

Dear Mr. Barry

In response to your well-written letter:
College will most certainly be the best time of your life, but only if you take full advantage of all that college life has to offer. By all means enjoy social activities, but if you fritter away your time partying and/or goofing off, you might just as well stay at home.

Instead of spending the time trying to find out who you really are (a form of navel contemplation), focus on what you wish to become. Decide on a goal and aim for it. I knew all through high school that I wanted to have a career in music. And then I worked as hard as I could to achieve that desire. As it turned out, although I have indeed had a career in music, it has often been in areas that were not expected by me. I have a niece who went into medicine expecting to specialize in ob/gyn and who has turned out to be a highly respected gastro-enterologist. The point here is that we each had a strong focus, and even though our areas of specialization shifted, we have ended up doing pretty much what we wanted to do. Most people are not that lucky.

Many of us have had high school girl friends that we have drifted away from, or have drifted away from us. Although some high school sweethearts have eventually married or settle down, I daresay that it more often turns out otherwise. At age 18, one is simply not ready to get tied down. Yes, at 18 it's easy to think you have it all figured out. I was once 18, too, and I have sometimes wished that I knew as much now as I thought I did at that age.

Yes, we are busy people, but the honesty of your letter intrigued me. I also wondered why you would write a faculty member at a music conservatory when you seem to have an enthusiasm for writing. (By the way, I don't recall hearing of anyone making a career of surfing. Fun, yes but as a career objective, uh-huh.)

I see from your C/V that you have an excellent academic record and are fortunate to have a pair of professionals for parents. You have a lot going for you. Good luck.

JOHN MORIARTY
NEW ENGLAND CONSERVATORY

Look Out and Network

"Be on the watch for those certain moments and certain people that come along and point you in a new direction. I think, for example, of the first time I met my friend and colleague Secretary Don Rumsfeld. It was back in the 1960's. He was a congressman, and I was interviewing for a fellowship in Washington, D.C. Congressman Rumsfeld agreed to interview me, but things didn't go all that smoothly—just 15 minutes later, I found myself back out in the hallway. Don's impression of me was that I was kind of a detached, impractical, academic type. And I thought he was a brash, cocky, young politician. And we were both right."

—DICK CHENEY,
VICE PRESIDENT OF THE UNITED STATES

"Whatever your ambitions, whatever the field you want to enter, if you want to play a game, go to where it's played. If you want to be a lawyer, go to law school. If you can't get into the best law school, get into the best one you can. . . ."

—CHRIS MATTHEWS, HOBART AND WILLIAM SMITH COLLEGES, 2004

"ABSOLUTELY. THOSE FOUR YEARS MAKE A BIG DIFFERENCE. YOU'LL EXPAND YOUR HORIZONS A DOZEN WAYS. THESE ARE THE MATURING YEARS TO LEARN AND ABSORB AS MUCH AS YOU CAN ABOUT EVERYTHING—ESPECIALLY IF YOU ARE A WRITER."

—REGIS PHILBIN, *Live with Regis and Kelly*

"I entered the University to become an electrical engineer! While there, I became a journalist. I left a position as city editor for a daily newspaper to take an advanced degree in history to make myself a better newsman. I eventually emerged with a doctorate. . . .

—DONALD DEWEY, DEAN OF UNIVERSITY'S SCHOOL OF NATURAL AND SOCIAL SCIENCES, CALIFORNIA STATE UNIVERSITY

"Free yourself from comparison. Just because someone has fancy sneakers doesn't mean they can run faster."

—Jon Bon Jovi, Monmouth University, 2001

"Setting a plan for life can be a good thing. It keeps you focused on the future, gives you a standard against which you can measure progress. Yet, I'll wager 10 years from now, many of you will find yourselves following a very different course all because of an opportunity that came out of the blue. . . ."

—DICK CHENEY, VICE PRESIDENT OF THE UNITED STATES

"THE TIME HAS COME FOR YOU TO DROP YOUR TAILS AND LEAVE THIS SWAMP."

—Kermit the Frog, Southampton College, 1996

LOOKING BACK . . .

■ PETER J. TALBOT
QUALITY MANAGER, GE CAPITAL BUSINESS
CREDIT SERVICE

Q: *What was the most important thing you learned in college? Why?*
A: Study what interests you, even in the least. A broad area of study is beneficial. The work/professional skills truly come through experience. Enjoy yourself and the time/experiences you have at college.

Q: *Did college help you to understand yourself? How?*
A: To some degree—helped focus my interests and assisted in deciding what professional field to pursue.

Q: *Did the college experience help you become the person you are today?*
A: Not really. It gave me the theoretical business background and understanding of business topics/functions;

Q: *Did you keep your high school friends?*
A: Some— but it is a definite two-way effort and not always easy to maintain connections through multiple relocations.

Q: *If you didn't go to college, did you ever regret it? Why?*
A: N/A-But I did serve in the military prior to college, and the experience strengthened my desires to obtain college education/degree.

August 9, 2004

Dear Mr. Barry:

Bravo! You are heading to college not thinking about your career or marriage or success (I assume you mean financial success) right now. That means you have a chance for a college experience in the very best sense of higher education, rather than purely vocation preparation. Use this time to discover how you can make a difference in the world!

At least for your freshman and sophomore years, please keep that open mind and explore ideas and options that you might choose to focus on in a major as an upperclassman. Get to know people who are different from you, so you can see yourself in the context of the many different people of the USA and the world. Yes, you've traveled, but college gives you a chance to make friends with many different people, not just meet them.

You will discover more clearly the ideas and values that make you who you are. That will happen through experiences in and out of the classroom. You have a very good chance to discover what you can contribute to the world through your career. Be prepared to work much harder than you are now expecting, as college professors at fine schools like Tulane — where the average SAT score for the 2003-2004 freshman class was1331 or 305 points above the national average—are demanding. College is not high school!

I went to a very fine liberal arts institution, Lawrence University in Wisconsin, and college was in fact one of the best times of my life. I too was an honors student in high school, but I also had a passion for learning, discovering and writing—so I could hardly wait to go to college. My education prepared me for a career and for a life by helping me discover a wider world, people with different ways of thinking—and what types of writing I was best suited for as a career. Special experiences such as service on the President's Student Advisory Board introduced me to working with college and university presidents – something I have done for many years that I certainly did not envision doing at the time.

Life is filled with serendipity—chance encounters, opportunities, and new people met. Stay open to seeing those opportunities for they may lead to careers, opportunities for service, friendships that you never dreamed of. You need to give your life direction, yet not such rigid direction that you pass by that door to a new skill, new friends, new career opportunities that let you use your talents to the fullest. That latter will give you the greatest satisfaction in life outside of your family.

Yes, I kept high school friends—a small group of us have corresponded with each other for more than 40 years, sharing life's joys and sorrows. That has meant a lot. You and your girlfriend will mature a lot in the next four years and both will meet many people. If you two are meant to be, it will work out.

Good luck. Please write at the end of your first semester and tell me what you think of college, okay?

Sincerely,

Barbara B. Petura
Associate Vice President
  for University Relations

"I do not recognize the person who entered college and the one who came out."

—KEN BURNS, Film Documentarist

"IF I HAD NEVER GONE TO COLLEGE, I NO DOUBT WOULD HAVE REGRETTED IT. COLLEGE STIMULATED ME INTELLECTUALLY, BUT ALSO PROVIDED ME WITH THE TOOLS AND SKILLS NECESSARY TO APPRECIATE LIFE AND ALL IT HAS TO OFFER."

—DR. ALBERT D. GRAHAM, JR., Director of Early Childhood & Federal/State Programs, Penns Grove-Carneys Point Regional School District

"Don't fear that silent room. Solitude will guide you if you remain strong of character."

—WALLY LAMB, Author, Connecticut College, 2003

Recipe for Life

"Listen to Mom and Dad—nobody cares about you more than they do. College is certainly not a prerequisite for success in life, and it won't take the place of self-confidence, positive attitude and hard work. But, put them all together and it could be dynamite.

—ANTON DELFORNO, JUSTON RECORDS

QUIET POWER, INC.

August 8, 2004

Dear Douglas,

It was nice to receive your letter regarding your entry into college. How did you select me?

I want to say that your writing is excellent. I am the author of 7 books, and I know a good write when I "See" one. Your future with written products looks great!

Your questions are excellent, yet each person is different. No two people are alike, just as each snowflake is unique. It sounds as if you have an incredibly good start with your high school record and achievements. Your educational experiences abroad are outstanding. Also, my son graduated from Princeton, and I truly believe it helped shape the person he is today.

Yes, my high school romances drifted away. Yet, I have many friends who married their high school sweetheart.

I do not think college helped make me the person I am today, yet the experiences in college all added into my life equation. As you move through life, look at everything as a learning experience. There are lots of bumps in the road, yet how you choose to see things can make the world of difference. There are the good times, the bad time, the tough times, etc. Always strive to do your best and know that you can do anything. I love this quote by Henry Ford, "Think you can, or think you can't, either way you'll be right."

Here's another critical point to remember. Busy people take the time to respond or act upon things that they determine are important. I hope I have answered your questions, and wish you continuous success.

Sincerely,

Karen Mantyla
President, Quiet Power, Inc.

"I CAN SAY, WITHOUT ANY RESERVATION, THAT EDUCATION, INCLUDING COLLEGE, IS A VITAL KEY TO GROWING INTO AN INDEPENDENT, SUCCESSFUL, GOOD CHARACTER ADULT."

—BERNIE SHAW, Sales Manager, Cherner Tyson Automotive Group

"I regrettably did not attend college. Even though there are a multitude of reasons for such, I to this day regret the missed experiences that only college can afford you."

—JOHN ISGETT, PRESIDENT, RACEWAY AUTOMOTIVE GROUP

"I VALUE EDUCATION; NOT GOING TO COLLEGE PLACES STRICT LIMITATIONS ON YOUR WORK AND YOUR FRIENDS—AND YOUR POTENTIAL FOR GROWTH AND DEVELOPMENT AS AN INDIVIDUAL."

—JOYCE LOGAN, Associate Professor, College of Education, University of Kentucky

Electives of Life

"But the unfortunate, yet truly exciting thing about your life, is that there is no core curriculum. The entire place is an elective. The paths are infinite and the results uncertain. . . . So if there's any real advice I can give you its this. College is something you complete. Life is something you experience. So don't worry about your grade, or the results or success. Success is defined in myriad ways, and you will find it, and people will no longer be grading you, but it will come from your own internal sense of decency."

—JON STEWART, WILLIAM AND MARY, 2004

"ALL UNIVERSITIES, AT THEIR BEST, TEACH THAT DEGREES AND HONORS ARE FAR FROM THE FULL MEASURE OF LIFE, NOR IS THAT MEASURE TAKEN IN WEALTH OR IN TITLES. WHAT MATTERS MOST ARE THE STANDARDS YOU LIVE BY, THE CONSIDERATION YOU SHOW OTHERS, AND THE WAY YOU USE THE GIFTS THAT YOU ARE GIVEN."

—PRESIDENT GEORGE W. BUSH, Yale University, 2001

"Never be afraid to roll up your sleeves, get down in the dirt, and commit, with passion and persistence, to accomplishing the task, or attaining the goal, you've set for yourself. Get involved and take what you've learned and use it to help make this a better world than the one that is waiting for you when you leave here today."

—KATHRYN S. FULLER, BROWN UNIVERSITY, 2004

"BEGIN YOUR NEXT GREAT PHASE OF YOUR LIFE BY GIVING, AND . . . CONTINUE AS YOU BEGIN. I THINK YOU'LL FIND IN THE END THAT YOU GOT FAR MORE THAN YOU EVER HAD, AND DID MORE GOOD THAN YOU EVER DREAMED."

—STEPHEN KING, Vassar College, 2001

Bravery on the Rocks

"Be brave enough to live life creatively. The creative is the place where no one else has ever been. It is not the previously known. You have to leave the city of your comfort and go into the wilderness of your intuition. You can't get there by bus, only by hard work and risk and by not quite knowing what you're doing, but what you'll discover will be wonderful. What you'll discover will be yourself."

—ALAN ALDA, CONNECTICUT COLLEGE, 1980

Growth

EVOLVE WITH EACH QUESTION

growth (noun):
the process of growing or developing
—*American Heritage Dictionary,* **3rd Edition**

"You will go outside of yourself and this will help you understand who you are—don't think too much!"

—NANCY LITTLE, SCHOOL DIRECTOR, NATIONAL ACADEMY SCHOOL OF FINE ARTS

The shape of my life has been determined by all of the experiences that I have had thus far. It's been dictated less by the choices I've made than my surroundings, my parents and friends. What will happen to me in these next years at college? Is this where I will become an adult, where the majority of my personality will be formed? Or, rather, will I build on what I already am, becoming a more mature form of myself? I want to grow, to change, but at the same time I want to be able to recognize the person I will become after college. Growing up is a hard prospect to face. I have to start to take responsibility for my own actions and accept any consequences. I want to think that this is what it means to be an adult, but I realize that in more ways than not I am still a kid, yearning for the opportunity to stay in bed lazily on a Sunday morning and have dad cook a huge breakfast.

What will happen when I leave college? I mean, will those four years be enough to mold me into a working, functioning part of society? Do I want to be a functioning part of society or do I want to define myself in a different way? Will the ideals I have now stay with me in a few short years, or will college life completely redefine my self and my expectations?

I start to realize that I cannot control what college will or will not do to me anymore than I can control the changing weather. The fact remains that I can only be true to myself as I go along. As much as I want to try to control the change and know that in four or five years I will be exactly where I'd predicted I'd be, somewhere along the line I realize that I just have to let go. Let control fly out of the window and just cruise through life, aware, yet passive, allowing things to happen as they will and learn and benefit from those experiences.

The more I think about it, the more I try to understand that changing is part of growing. No matter how much I try to resist the change, sometimes I need it in order to become what I want to be. In order to get to the future I have to allow myself to be taken by the current, always watchful of how far I'm drifting, yet allowing myself to sail easily along unobstructed by struggle and resistance.

"If nothing else, studying so many different things for so many years has shown me how much more I have to learn."

—LAURA EWALD, Professor, Murray State University

"As one grows older, matures and experiences life throughout the years, it helps one to have an even better understanding of oneself, which is a never-ending, ongoing process."

—DR. ALBERT D. GRAHAM, JR., DIRECTOR OF EARLY CHILDHOOD & FEDERAL/STATE PROGRAMS, PENNS GROVE-CARNEYS POINT REGIONAL SCHOOL DISTRICT

"It is perfectly OK to be helped along, but if you really aspire to be a [success], you must learn to continue to strive for excellence. Learn to do what ought to be done, when it should be done, whether you like it or not."

—ROY HALEY, CEO, WESCO DISTRIBUTION, INC.

COMMONWEALTH *of* VIRGINIA

Department of the Treasury

JODY M. WAGNER
TREASURER OF VIRGINIA

P.O. BOX 1879
RICHMOND, VIRGINIA 23218-1879

August 13, 2004

Mr. Douglas Barry

Dear Douglas:

First, congratulation on your admission to Tulane University! That is a wonderful institution, which I am sure you will enjoy.

Douglas, you wrote me inquiring as to whether or not I thought it was worth attending college. Unequivocally – yes! As I am sure your mother and father will concur, your college experience will broaden your mind, expand your horizons, and significantly enhance your opportunities for.success. I have four children, two of whom have already engaged in the college experience. The first one has graduated and is going on to pursue a Masters, and the second is entering his sophomore year in college. For them, I can assure you, the college experience has been most worthwhile.

I understand your reluctance, but strongly recommend that you proceed to New Orleans.

With best wishes for your success, I remain

Sincerely yours,

Jody M. Wagner

LOOKING BACK . . .

■ JANET ROBINSON
EVP/COO, THE NEW YORK TIMES COMPANY

Q: *What was the most important thing you learned in college? Why?*
A: 1. Develop a love of learning.
Realize how strong interpersonal skills are gifts.
Never dream small dreams—Be confident in your abilities but humble.

Q: *Did college help you to understand yourself? How?*
A: Yes. I grew into an adult during my college years as I developed a love of learning. I also began to realize what I did and did not want to do. College is the time to do that.

Q: *Did the college experience help you become the person you are today?*
A: Yes, my college experiences helped me develop personal and professional goals that helped me understand what matters like education, family, integrity and character.

Q: *Did you keep your high school friends?*
A: Yes, I have to this day. Old friends give you perspective.

Q*: If you didn't go to college, did you ever regret it? Why?*
A: I attended college and enjoyed every minute.

"HERE'S MY LIST:

1. FIRST AND FOREMOST IS A SOLID WORK ETHIC. MY PARENTS RAN THE
   LOCAL WESTERN AUTO STORE, SO I WAS INTRODUCED EARLY TO THE
   IMPORTANCE OF WORK.
2. THE SECOND IS THE WILLINGNESS TO TAKE ON REASONABLE RISKS. . . .
3. FINALLY, GETTING A GOOD WELL-ROUNDED EDUCATION. KEEP THOSE
   GRADES UP; STAY INVOLVED IN EXTRACURRICULAR ACTIVITIES. YOU
   LEARN A LOT OF LEADERSHIP SKILLS THAT WAY."

—EARNEST W. DEAVENPORT, Jr., Chairman and CEO, Eastman Chemical Company

"Your letter reminded me of what my life was like during that time. As eager as I was for adventure, I felt as though I was moving toward a cliff and was about to be pushed off. . . . Nobody is going to be able to offer you the comfort you are seeking because the experience is different for everyone. Yes, college will be different from high school. Don't worry. It's good. It's part of becoming your own person. It all gets better."

—BRIAN COLBATH, INSTRUCTOR, PROJECTS PLUS, INC.

Dear Douglas,

I am not really sure why you have asked ME to participate in your 'questionnaire' or how you came across my details...so, an answer to my questions sent by you to my email address** would be appreciated in return for me answering your questions!!

Q1: The most important thing I learned in college (by college, I assume you mean university??..which is where we go to in the UK at 18)
A: Not to judge and stereotype other students and the teaching staff by the very juvenile and distorted opinions which I, coming from a provincial working class city where I had never met people from better off families than me, held at the time.

Q2: Did college help me to understand myself?
A: Yes, but only after I graduated and had been in employment for some considerable time.

Q3: Did the college experience help me become the person I am today?
A: No, not in any major way, apart from improving my education, enhancing my political awareness and widening my circle of friends. The events which really changed my life and made me the person I am today came long after I left college and arose from entirely unforeseeable events which challenged me in ways which college never did.

Q4: Did I keep some high school friends?
A: Sadly, no...

I daresay my answers to your formal questionnaire less than you had hoped for, but do not despair. . . .

You ask whether college is going to be the best time of you life!! The answer is undoubtedly Yes…compared to the life you have had up to this time, but probably not compared to the life you will have…after college.

Will college be any different to High School? Definitely yes…especially if you go far from home to another part of the country (as you should) where you cannot run home at the first sign of trouble...this is when you really begin growing up on your own without parents to guide you.

Drifting away from your girlfriend… if you are a long way from home and can only communicate by phone, email, letter, etc., then I think you will find it much harder to sustain the new relationship as you will find new friends who don't have any connection to your current GF; you will get used to their company, share experiences with them etc. from which your GF will be excluded. She too will experience the same separation from you, either because she has gone to a different college or stayed at home. It's all part of life's constant movement. Did I love someone in school and lose them in college?? No, I didn't but I did lose someone I loved in the university when I graduated.

Take care of yourself

Colin Parry

"One of your hallmarks as a generation from my point of view may be an admirable, droll skepticism. You do not want to be easily sold or too easily sold to."

—ROBERT PINSKY, Stanford University, 1999

"I SAY YOU CAN'T STAND IF YOU'VE GOT TOO MUCH MUCK IN YOUR HEAD. LET IT GO AND DANCE THROUGH LIFE. AFTER ALL, IN THE BIG PICTURE, WE'RE ALL JUST PART OF THE HARMONY CALLED THE UNIVERSE."

—YOKO ONO, Maine College of Art, 2003

"THERE ARE SO MANY WONDERFUL THINGS AHEAD OF YOU. HANG IN THERE. DON'T GIVE UP. FIGHT THE GOOD FIGHT. IT WON'T BE EASY, BUT IT WILL BE WORTH IT."

—KELSEY GRAMMER, University of Massachusetts Amherst, 2001

The Keys to Courage

"You have achieved your goal, and now you are ready to begin another chapter. Now you really start real life. Real life may be more complicated. It is bound to face some unhappy things and hindrance and obstacles, complications. So it is important to have determination and optimism and patience. If you lack patience, even when you face some small obstacle, you lose courage."

—TENZIN GYATSO, HIS HOLINESS THE 14TH DALAI LAMA, EMORY UNIVERSITY, 1998

"If you go through life convinced that your way is always best, all the new ideas in the world will pass you by."

—AKIO MORITA, Founder, Sony Corporation

"IF THESE ARE INDEED THE BEST YEARS OF YOUR LIFE, YOU DO NOT HAVE MY CONDOLENCES BECAUSE THERE IS NOTHING, BELIEVE ME, MORE SATIS-FYING, MORE GRATIFYING THAN TRUE ADULTHOOD."

—TONI MORRISON, Author, Wellesly College, 2004

"Real courage and bravery is not as some people think a lack of fear. . . . Courage is about being able to feel that fear and then going ahead and doing what you believe is right anyways, even if you are afraid."

—RUDY GIULIANI, STONEY CREEK HIGH SCHOOL, SHANKSVILLE, PENNSYLVANIA, 2002

LOOKING BACK . . .

■ **KEN BURNS**
FLORENTINE FILMS

Q: *What was the most important thing you learned in college? Why?*
A: To know is not enough. Understanding is key. College provides the discernment to know the difference.

Q: *Did college help you to understand yourself? How?*
A: Yes. It reminded me to question assumptions that limited me.

Q: *Did the college experience help you become the person you are today?*
A: Yes. I do not recognize the person who entered college and the person who came out.

Q: *Did you keep your high school friends?*
A: Yes, many of them.

PRESIDENT

Dear Douglas:

I appreciate the fact that you are standing at a critical juncture at this point in your life—right on the crossroads between youth and adulthood.

You have absorbed all the influences that you were able to from your hometown. Now is the time to take the next formative step in your personal development. College, a unique experience allows you the time and personal space to develop your intellect, expand your interests and generally shaped your worldview. By coming in to contact with other young people from all over the nation and all over the globe, you will be better positioned to carve out your place in this complex internationally linked world.

This four year educational exploration will serve as a template for further professional and personal growth. By all means, I urge you to seize this intellectually stimulating and character developing opportunity. By the way, it is also a lot of fun!

Best wishes for some success,

Ella for J.K.

Ella for J.K.

901 15th Street, NW • Suite 700 • Washington, DC 20005 • 202-712-3000 • 202-712-3001 fax

www.JohnKerry.com

Paid for by John Kerry for President, Inc.

Contributions or gifts to John Kerry for President, Inc. are not deductible for federal income tax purposes.

2

Remember yourself, from the days when you were younger and rougher and wilder, more scrawl than straight line. Remember all of yourself, the flaws and faults as well as the many strengths."

—ANNA QUINDLEN, MOUNT HOLYOKE COLLEGE, 1999

"LIVING A MORAL LIFE IN AN INDIFFERENT WORLD IS LIKELY TO BE MORE DIFFICULT THAN YOU CAN IMAGINE."

—CHRISTOPHER REEVE, Ohio State University, 2003

"I'LL BET YOUR VALUES ARE ALREADY FORMED. NOW YOU DISCOVER THEM FOR YOURSELF, TREASURE THEM AND HANG ON TO THEM. THEY ARE YOUR ANCHOR, YOUR NORTH STAR. YOU WON'T FIND THEM IN A BOOK. YOU'LL FIND THEM IN YOUR SOUL."

—ANNE M. MULCAHY, Chairman & CEO, Xerox Corporation

"Get out of your way. You can spend your life tripping on yourself, you can also spend your life tripping yourself up."

—SUZAN-LORI PARKS, Playwright, Mount Holyoke College, 2001

"LEARN TO UNDERSTAND AND TRUST YOUR HEAD AND YOUR HEART. INTUITION CANNOT BE LEARNED IN BOOKS AND TAKES TIME."

—ROY ELLIOTT, CHAIRMAN, President & CEO, Zimmer Holdings, Inc.

"Love what you do. Get good at it. Competence is a rare commodity in this day and age. And let the chips fall where they may."

—JON STEWART, William and Mary, 2004

Sept. 7, 2004

Dear Douglas:

I certainly enjoyed hearing from you and learning of your concerns as you prepare to enter college. Let me start by saying, you have certainly had a wonderful basis for doing well in college. I have no doubts you will thoroughly enjoy the experience and any little doubts that might creep in to your mind, especially early on, will, I'm sure, be readily put to rest.

You see Douglas, I never did go to college. I cannot really say whether I regret it or not, since I never experienced any of the facets of college life. Nevertheless, I had a very interesting life (in the entertainment business -- since I was three years old) and have loved every moment of it. I learned a great deal from so many of the wonderful people I met and worked with through the years, and to this day, I maintain many of the friendships I made during my early years in elementary school.

There is no doubt you will grow as a person during your college years. You will make many decisions on your own, etc., but I'd venture to say your parents will always be close by as your support.

I wish you all the best in the wonderful experiences upon which you are about to embark -- make the best of it all and you will do just fine. Blessings to you and thank you again for having written.

Lots of love,

Rose Marie

RM/dw

"IMITATE NO ONE.
YOUR UNIQUENESS—YOUR AUTHENTICITY—
IS YOUR STRENGTH."

—Wally Lamb, Author, Connecticut College, 2003

"IF YOU HAVE TO CHOOSE CHARACTER OR INTELLIGENCE—IN A FRIEND OR IN A CANDIDATE—CHOOSE CHARACTER. INTELLIGENCE WITHOUT CHARACTER IS DANGEROUS, BUT CHARACTER WITHOUT INTELLIGENCE ONLY SLOWS DOWN A GOOD RESULT."

—GLORIA STEINEM, Tufts University, 1987

Building Blocks

"Life offers many challenges and opportunities. A reputation among your colleagues for integrity, fairness and teamwork are the attributes of a successful person. Hard work, planning and determination will enable you to take full advantage of offers that may come your way."

—THOMAS J. SLOCUM, SVP CORPORATE
COMMUNICATIONS, DELTA AIR LINES

AR P® Laboratories

May 5, 2003

500 Chipeta Way • Salt Lake City, Utah 84108

Douglas Barry

Voorhees, NJ 08043

Dear Douglas:

Thank you for your letter asking me to answer two questions regarding the role of the leader.

I am impressed with your resume. You are well-rounded, and your interest in learning about different cultures and spending time in Europe to broaden your education are all very positive.

I would like to make the following comments regarding your two questions: first of all, there was no specific turning point that brought me down the path to become a leader. I was brought up in a family where my father and my brothers, from early on, had been in leadership positions, and I followed in their footsteps. As a teenager, I was a leader of various sports teams in Europe, both in skiing as well as in various summer sports. At the age of 16, I spent a year in the United States, from Norway, as an exchange student. This maturing experience gave me confidence and an edge up on my fellow students when I returned to Norway. I was elected president of all the four high schools in my hometown. Following medical school in Edinburgh, Scotland, I came to the United States where I did my residency training in hematopathology. My first job at the University of Utah was to be in a leadership position as Director of their Hematology Laboratory. From then until now, I have gone from one leadership position to another.

I don't think that I have ever consciously strived to be a leader—it has been more of being offered leadership positions. You don't just go out and say "I want to be a leader." You have to earn it and show you are capable.

You asked what do you need to know beyond books and academics to become a leader. Books and academics give you credibility, but that does not necessarily make you a leader. A good leader is someone who can set aside their own ego and get pleasure in seeing others succeed by creating an environment which is conducive to success for those that you lead. It is about caring and showing compassion and not leading by power. It is not necessarily expertise and experience which are important, it's what is referred to as emotional intelligence that counts.

In today's environment, successful leaders are those that believe in a team approach and who surround themselves with people better than they are, encourage honest feedback and innovation, and have an open-door policy.

I strongly believe that if you take care of your employees they will take care of your bottom-line.

I hope this has been useful to you. We have in the last few years seen examples of poor leadership where the CEO only cared for himself/herself. This has deservedly given the position of CEO a bad reputation, but I believe that there are many more good CEO's than bad ones.

I wish you much success and happiness in the future. I would be interested in knowing what you end up doing.

Sincerely,

Carl R. Kjeldsberg, M.D.
President and CEO

CRK/rmk

Stellar Success Tips

"1. Take a chance on a position that excites you and will accelerate your learning.
2. Work hard at every assignment, always do more than what is asked for.
3. Be more curious about how things work . . . focus as much on process as outcome."

—PETER SODERBURG, President & CEO,
Welch Allyn

"Last night, I saw, I was so inspired by the performance of all of the students. And the edge is your friend. See, when you have your tools in order, you can go to that edge, and jump off, and just fly."

—DIANNE REEVES, BERKLEE COLLEGE OF MUSIC, 2003

"You can be catalysts for change. Ubiquitous as it seems today, change is not some natural process, overwhelming, inexorable and beyond our control. Change is the result of human ideas and actions—the cumulative consequence of the visions, needs, fears and dreams of six billion people like ourselves around the world."

—QUEEN NOOR OF JORDAN,
PRINCETON UNIVERSITY, 2000

"WE MUST, IN OUR DAILY LIVES, STRUGGLE TO KEEP OUR CONSCIOUSNESS GROWING."

—OLIVER STONE, UC Berkeley, 1997

Secretary to
HIS HOLINESS THE DALAI LAMA

July 31, 2004

Mr. Douglas Barry

Dear Mr. Douglas Barry,

This is to acknowledge receipt of your letter addressed to His Holiness the Dalai Lama dated July 19, 2004. I am enclosing here a signed card containing a printed message of His Holiness.

Best wishes,

Yours sincerely,

Tenzin Geyche Tethong

Thekchen Choeling, Mcleod Ganj 176219, Dharamsala, Himachal Pradesh, India

A Message from H.H. the Dalai Lama

Never Give up
No matter what is going on
Never Give up
Develop the heart
Too much energy in your country
is spent developing the mind
instead of the heart
Be compassionate
Not just to your friends
but to everyone
Be compassionate
Work for peace
in your heart and in the world
Work for peace
and I say again
Never Give up
No matter what is happening
No matter what is going on around you
Never Give up.

H.H. the XIVth Dalai Lama

Tough Stuff

"The hardest things in life, you'll soon learn, are the small things. The big decisions are the easy ones. It's the day-to-day trouble of having to choose between confronting the petty corruption around you or letting things slide, going with the flow. That's the tough stuff. And how you decide will show whether you have the right stuff."

—CHRIS MATTHEWS,
HOBART AND WILLIAM SMITH COLLEGES, 2004

"IF YOUR SUCCESS IS NOT ON YOUR OWN TERMS, IF IT LOOKS GOOD TO THE WORLD BUT DOES NOT FEEL GOOD IN YOUR HEART, IT IS NOT SUCCESS AT ALL. REMEMBER THE WORDS OF LILY TOMLIN: 'IF YOU WIN THE RAT RACE, YOU'RE STILL A RAT.'"

—ANNA QUINDLEN, Mount Holyoke College, 1999

"Bend down once in a while and smell a flower."

—RUSSELL BAKER, Connecticut College, 1995

"When you don't act, you act. When you don't vote, you vote. When you accept the loony logic of some of the left that there is no political value in supporting the lesser of two evils, you open the door to the greater evil. That's what happens when you despair, you open the door to evil, and evil is always happy to enter, sit down. . . . Act. Organize. It's boring but do it, the world ends if you don't."

—TONY KUSHNER, VASSAR COLLEGE, 2002

LOOKING BACK . . .

■ HARLEY JANE KOZAK
NOVELIST

Q: *What was the most important thing you learned in college? Why?*
A: That everything counts. The smallest action has meaning. Because life is short.

Q: *Did college help you to understand yourself? How?*
A: Yes. It exposed me to wise, dedicated, knowledgeable, artistic people who wanted to help me.

Q: *Did the college experience help you become the person you are today?*
A: Absolutely.

Q: *Did you keep your high school friends?*
A: Yes.

Takeoff

PREPARE FOR THE RIDE OF YOUR LIFE

take.off (noun):
the act of leaving the ground
—*American Heritage Dictionary,* **3rd Edition**

"Dreams can come true. Set your goal for what-ever you want and go for it."

—JOHN TRAVOLTA, ACTOR

The plane is fueled and ready for takeoff. As the monstrous bird taxies and roars down the runway at Philadelphia International Airport my dad leans over and says, "This is the last time you'll see home until Christmas." I glance out of the window onto the city where I went to school for four years, staring at an amazing, rising sun illuminating the glass skyscrapers. The plane lifts higher into the sky, drifting further away from home with every inch it travels. I wonder about where my summer went, why I am on this plane, and more importantly, what is waiting for me in New Orleans.

I can't help but think that home may become more important to me when I am away from it than when I am in it. It's impossible for me to pinpoint what home means to me. The further the plane travels the more I understand that the pang of pain in my heart is actually my yearning to go back to where I was. I know all the roads, all the places to go. I have a car, friends, familiarity, and a solid and well-styled life. All of that— my life, the places I go, the people I hang out with—is going to change very soon, and I will eventually go home to find that it will have changed without me there to observe and be a part of it. This fact brings a certain alienation and sadness. I want to be a part of everything all at once— go to college but not miss a beat at home, stay with all my friends and make totally new ones—and reserve a seat everywhere I go.

I remember surfing during a hurricane after dad said, "Don't you dare go out there alone." It wasn't one of my finest moments but there I was staring ten feet of water in the face. I paddled to catch the face of the wave and only remember feeling like it was sweeping me away. I came crashing down in a whirlpool of foam and water, struggling, gasping for air as I climbed for the surface. I looked back at shore, grabbed my board and decided to go in to catch my breath. I learned a lesson that day and was beaten by the surf without a struggle. In a way it was the ocean's way of letting me know that I was still a visitor; that I could never master the unpredictable, expansive element of the sea. I know that going to college is going to be like wiping out, going under, and then coming up for air, but I'm ready for the challenge. For a few weeks my head will be under water as I try to find my place, my niche, the surface where I can finally breathe.

What is awaiting me in New Orleans? Maybe I can expect failure in school, heartbreak, and homesickness. Maybe I can expect to change completely, fall in love with the city and never leave. Maybe going to school is going to be the best thing to happen to me. Maybe I'm going to transfer. All I know for sure as the plane carries me ever so far away from home is that I have lived my life until this very point and, now, with all my apprehensions and insecurities, I am ready to move on and take the next step in my growth. Other than that, I have absolutely no clue what's in store for me in the Big Easy.

"Smile. You're one of the luckiest people in the world. You're living in America. Enjoy it."

—RUSSELL BAKER, Connecticut College, 1995

"AFTER ALL THIS SCHOOLING, YOU SHOULD KNOW HOW TO COOK. SO COOK AWAY AND GIVE US THE GOOD STUFF FOR A CHANGE. PLEASE. WE NEED IT."

—BILLY JOEL, Berklee College of Music, 1993

"I urge you to seize this intellectually stimulating and character developing opportunity. By the way, it is also a lot of fun."

—JOHN KERRY, United States Senator

BOB DOLE

September 30, 2004

Dear Douglas,

Thank you for your recent letter regarding your upcoming freshman year at Tulane.

Throughout your college years, you will undoubtedly be challenged in many respects – intellectually, morally, and socially. Take these opportunities as learning experiences. With each new struggle comes a new realization of your strengths.

Strive to achieve your goals through self-determination, yet always hold on to your core values and character. Life may present you with difficult situations, but you will weather any storm with a healthy attitude and a good dose of confidence.

Good luck at Tulane, and keep up the good work!

God Bless America,

BOB DOLE

You can do it!!

LOOKING BACK . . .

■ LAURA EWALD
PROFESSOR, MURRAY STATE UNIVERSITY

Q: *What was the most important thing you learned in college? Why?*
A: There are No shortcuts. Cramming after weeks of procrastination might get you through tomorrow's exam, but it won't help you next week, next month, or next year when you need what wasn't actually learned the first time around. Finish all work to completion on your own. The next time, things will be easier as you build on your personal knowledge base and successes.

Q: *Did college help you to understand yourself? How?*
A: I came to identify myself as a conservative independent thinker. After some 14 years of professors at 6 public institutions in 3 states, I learned that information is not knowledge, and knowledge only sometimes leads to wisdom. Trust the writers and thinkers who are respected by those whom you know and trust and respect, not just anyone who happens to have a lot of letters after his or her name.

Q: *Did the college experience help you become the person you are today?*
A: If nothing else, studying so many different things for so many years has shown me how much more I have to learn. I would guess that is why I became a reference librarian, the one profession that allows me to spend my days constantly asking—and finding answers to—new questions.

Q: *Did you keep your high school friends?*

A: Not for the most part. I do have one friend with whom I'm still in contact occasionally. We've known each other since the 8th grade, and though we don't talk for months at a time, when we do communicate, it seems as though we last spoke just yesterday. Of course we did "hang out" together in community theater the better part of 10 years after we graduated from high school, which probably has a lot more to do with our remaining in touch. Come to think of it, before I moved out-of-state, I had more friendships with parents of my high school classmates—and teacher—than actual classmates, oddly enough.

"LET YOURSELF RE-GRADUATE EVERY FOUR YEARS. CELEBRATE WHAT YOU HAVE DONE. ADMIT WHAT YOU ARE NOT DOING. THINK ABOUT WHAT IS IMPORTANT TO YOU AND MAKE SOME CHANGES. IF YOU GIVE YOURSELF A CHANCE TO MOVE ON, YOU CAN DO ANYTHING."

—CATHY GUISEWITE, Cartoonist, University of Michigan, 1994

"There are a lot of bumps in the road, yet how you choose to see things can make the world of difference."

—KAREN MANTYLA, President, Quiet Powers, Inc.

"It's true, I dropped out of college to start Microsoft, but I was at Harvard for three years before dropping out, and I would love to have the time to go back. As I've said before, nobody should drop out of college unless they believe they face an opportunity of a lifetime. And even then they should reconsider."

—BILL GATES, CHAIRMAN, MICROSOFT CORPORATION

Enjoy the Journey

"Don't confuse passion with success. Passion is the joy of getting there. Success can be a trap. I think this country and our culture glorifies and defies the goddess Success to the point that whenever we try and fail, we hear our own inner voices say, 'Shame on you." If there is any shame, it is in the fact that we inflict such heavy punishment on ourselves."

—Neil Simon, playwright,
Williams College, 1984

KENNY ROGERS

Dear Douglas,

Thanks so much for your letter of inquiry about the benefits of college. I think the fact that you would bother to write and ask these questions speaks volumes for who you are and your potential for success.

Let me tell you, first of all, that college can and should be one of the most wonderful and memorable times of your life. On the assumption that you take everything I say as strictly my opinion, I will offer it.

In high school there are no options—you go to class. In college, professors could care less whether you show up or not. College allows *your choices* to dictate *your consequences*. I will tell you what I told my son Christopher. One of the most important things a college degree does is tell a future employer "I have discipline . . . I didn't quit when I could have."

Douglas, I have great respect for anyone who goes to the trouble to seek out other people's advice. I give you permission to use what I've told you as an outsider's opinion, but I better not find out you told your mom and dad you're not going to college because of me.

The best piece of advice my mom gave me was "*find a job you love and you'll never work a day in you life.*" I wish that for you and congratulations on being accepted to Tulane University.

Your friend,

Kenny Rogers

"AS YOU LOOK AHEAD TO THE CHALLENGES THAT LIFE SURELY WILL PRES-
ENT, KEEP IN MIND THAT THERE IS MUCH ABOUT WHICH TO BE OPTIMISTIC.
THE WORLD IS RIPE WITH OPPORTUNITY FOR THOSE WHO WORK HARD, GET
AN EDUCATION AND PLAY BY THE RULES."

—George W. Bush, President of the United States

"THIS IS YOUR TIME: THE 21ST CENTURY. THE MILLENNIUM. IT IS YOURS TO SHAPE AND MASTER."

—TOM BROKAW, Connecticut College, 1996

Douglas:

The name is the same, but I'm not the Bernie Shaw you think I am.

However, I can speak from experience, having coached three children through college and career starts: I can say, without any reservation, that <u>education</u> including college was the vital key to their growing into independent, successful, <u>good character adults</u>.

So stay with it and good luck.

Sincerely,

Bernie Shaw
Sales Manager, Cherner Tyson Automotive Group

"I BELIEVE THAT IF YOU CAN LEARN TO FOCUS ON WHAT YOU HAVE, YOU WILL ALWAYS SEE THAT THE UNIVERSE IS ABUNDANT AND YOU WILL HAVE MORE. IF YOU CONCENTRATE AND FOCUS IN YOUR LIFE ON WHAT YOU DON'T HAVE, YOU WILL NEVER HAVE ENOUGH. BE GRATEFUL."

—Oprah Winfrey, Wellesley College, 1997

"If I had to go back, and do everything over, I'd do it again. With everything that's been wrong with my life; with everything that's been good; with all the mistakes, all the problems."

—RAY BRADBURY, CALTECH, 2000

"NO MATTER WHAT IS HAPPENING, NO MATTER WHAT IS GOING ON AROUND YOU, NEVER GIVE UP."

—HH The XIVth Dalai Lama

The Gift that Keeps Giving

"The turning point for me took place the day I graduated high school. I had not planned to go to college. My parents were 1st generation immigrants without a high school education. No relatives ever went to college. My grandfather came up, with tears in his eyes, gave me a hug and an envelope. It contained a few hundred dollars. He said he came to America to create a better life for his family, and I was the first with the ability to attend college. He taught me a lesson about responsibility and the rest is history."

—JON A. BOSCIA, CHAIRMAN & CEO, LINCOLN FINANCIAL CORP.

"In addition to increasing knowledge, which provided a foundation for graduate work, living independently away from home in a new environment helped me in the transition to adulthood and maturity for making decisions about my future."

—JOYCE LOGAN, ASSOCIATE PROFESSOR, COLLEGE OF EDUCATION, UNIVERSITY OF KENTUCKY

"LIKE THE GREEKS OF OLD, THERE ARE THREE IMPORTANT PARTS TO OUR LIFE: THE PHYSICAL, THE INTELLECTUAL AND THE SPIRITUAL. THEY ARE SOMEWHAT LIKE A THREE-LEGGED STOOL. THE TRICK IS TO KEEP ALL THREE LEGS IN BALANCE."

—DR. MARK P. MALKOVICH, General Director, Newport Music Festival

"None of us, no matter our age, history, or condition, had anything handed to us. We have to do it ourselves, and God only knows what we can, each of us, do for ourselves."

—JAMES EARL JONES, ITHICA COLLEGE, 2002

LOOKING BACK . . .

■ ANTON DELFORNO
JUSTON RECORDS

Q: *What was the most important thing you learned in college? Why?*
A: What I didn't want to do. Because you're exposed to different things and you begin to pick and choose—Also, it's like a social meeting ground of experiences which may be helpful later on.

Q: *Did college help you to understand yourself? How?*
A: Not really— was lucky—I already knew what I wanted to do by then and was very focused.

Q: *Did the college experience help you become the person you are today?*
A: A little maybe to the extent that you become a product of your environment. But it's sort of temporary. It sort of fades away as you enter the real world.

Q: *Did you keep your high school friends?*
A: Yes—not all but some as everyone sets out to make their own way in life, you drift away, you lose some, you gain others.

In closing: Listen to your Mom and Dad, nobody cares about you more than them. College is certainly not a pre-requisite for success in life and it won't take the place of self-confidence, positive attitude and hard work. But put them all together, it would be dynamite. It could bring you a little extra time if you don't know what you want to do yet. Maybe something there will attract you (besides girls) and concerning girls, when the right one comes along, you won't "drift apart". So don't go thinking some of those insecure thoughts I detect in your letter and forget about being too comfortable at home—you're a big boy now—old enough to be fighting in Iraq—think about that! I tell my boys the same thing—just get out there and do something—things will fall into place. Keep your self-confidence and go where your heart leads. I could go on but I think you get the idea.

Good luck and maybe I'll see you at one of my concerts some day.

"THERE IS NOT A LOT OF WISDOM—NOT REALLY—BUT THERE IS DISCOV-
ERY. AND WHAT YOU WILL PROBABLY DISCOVER WILL BE WHAT IS THE
TRUEST OF THE THINGS YOU ALREADY KNOW."

—LORRIE MOORE, St. Lawrence University, 2004

**"This is the hard work of your life in the world,
to make it all up as you go along, to acknowledge
the introvert, the clown, the artist, the reserved,
the distraught, the goofball, the thinker."**

—Anna Quindlen, Mount Holyoke College, 1999

*"Make the world before you a better one by going into it with all
boldness. You are up to it and you are fit for it; you deserve it and
if you make your own best contribution, the world before you will
become a bit more deserving of you."*

—SEAMUS HEANEY, UNIVERSITY OF
NORTH CAROLINA, 1996

Where the Heart is

"Love your work. If you always put your heart into everything you do, you really can't lose. If your heart is in it, you'll probably succeed, and if it isn't in it, you probably won't succeed. But the reason you can't lose is that whether you wind up making a lot of money or not, you will have had a wonderful time, and no one will ever be able to take that away from you. I want to tell you everything. I want to squeeze things great and small into this lingering good-bye. I want to tell you to keep laughing."

—ALAN ALDA, CONNECTICUT COLLEGE, 1980

Aim High

Above all, get out there and take part in the life of the university; much of what you learn here about leadership takes place in the classroom as well as in co- and extra- curricular activities. You will be enjoying life in a rich cultural mix of people and ideas and beliefs. Listen, learn and discern. From that, leadership will grow. Set high standards for yourself and don't be satisfied with anything other than your best effort. My hero, Teddy Roosevelt, gave us all sage advice: 'Keep your eyes on the stars,' he said. 'And keep your feet on the ground.'"

—SCOTT S. COWEN, TULANE UNIVERSITY, 2004

August 4, 2004

Dear Mr. Barry –

Thank you for writing to me, and I must say it is one of the first such letters to come my way.

You ask me whether or not I would advise a young person to go to college and I unhesitatingly say **ABSOLUTELY**. If you have parents who can help you financially, or you have some other means that allow you to go – you will be a step ahead of the game for several reasons. Probably the most practical reason is because a college degree is as necessary for job applications in this day and age, as a high school diploma was in my day. However, for other reasons college gives a person the chance to explore many subjects and topics, that might lead to a long term career. Not to mention the faculty inspiration that, again, might lead you to explore something you might not have explored otherwise. You will go outside of yourself and this will help you understand who you are – don't think too much!

I learned so much in college I cannot begin to describe it. For one thing, I took one year of Shakespeare and read everything he wrote – for that alone it was worth going. I had a fantastic Professor. Personally, I transferred from a state school in Ohio, after two years, to a larger private University after I had decided on a major. I met my husband in college. In fact, after my husband received a Ph.D in art history here in New York, I went back to Queens College and received a Masters degree.

So, go for it. Tulane sounds great, and you will be in a great town, New Orleans. I left a boyfriend, but it worked out okay. Take the risk, and make the leap and I believe you will not regret a moment.

Good luck,

Nancy Little
School Director

"What I have learned is that you will have plenty of time for life's many experiences in work and relationships and to take time to enjoy what has been offered."

—JOHN ISGETT, President, Raceway Automotive Group

"Education will prepare you for anything in life—honesty is one of the primary ingredients and necessary ingredients in life—and a sincere love of what you are doing is the fuel that makes it all run. . . ."

—SUMMERFIELD K. JOHNSON, JR., CEO, COCA COLA ENTERPRISES

"Remember: there's a great country out there. Take it."

—ROGER ROSENBLATT, Brigham Young University, 1998

Remain Optimistic

"Hope isn't a choice, it's a moral obligation, it's a human obligation, it's an obligation to the cells in your body, hope is a function of those cells, it's a bodily function the same as breathing and eating and sleeping; hope is not naïve, hope grapples endlessly with despair. Real vivid powerful thunderclap hope, like the soul, is at home in darkness, is divided; but lose your hope and you lose your soul, and you don't want to do that, trust me . . . you shouldn't be careless about it."

—TONY KUSHNER, Vassar College, 2002

Afterword

The sun is peeking through the window of my dorm, and through a tear in the sheets that surround my bunk bed. My roommate, Tyler, is three days gone and the room is quieter than it usually is. I've slept a total of three hours, spending most of the night saying my good-byes to the friends I've made in my first semester at school. As I stare at my luggage piled on my emptied desk, I start to wonder about what has happened to me, about how I've changed since the summer. Am I the same person as I was just four months ago? Will home be the same to me once I get there? I rouse myself from reflection and get slowly out of my bed (my makeshift fort of spare sheets and blankets) and throw on a nearly clean pair of jeans. I open my door and my sleep-deprived friend Vince stands on the other side with car keys in his hand. "You ready to go?"

I came to college not truly understanding what I was heading for. I knew I wanted to gain some sort of knowledge that went beyond books or class-rooms, but I could never pinpoint exactly what that was. The letters I received, and all the commencement speeches I read, gave me real good advice, but the truth is that all the advice in the world could never have prepared me for college. And it's not just school that I was preparing for. I was leaving home for the first time, a shaggy-haired surfer from New Jersey who had no place being in a city like New Orleans. Yet I found my way there anyway. I left my friends, my family, and all those familiar things that one tends to take for granted during the daily grind in the hometown. I made new friends, adopted a new routine, and formed a "home" in a place that was as foreign to me as the moon.

The person I thought I was changed before my very eyes at college. I mean, I was still Doug, in every weird and ridiculous way that I could have possibly been, but I was learning that there was more to me than what I originally thought. There were untapped emotions, vices, and talents that I had never seen before, that my teenage years at home had never shed light on. I also began to understand how much I didn't understand. The clarity I had hoped for from college never came and I was perhaps even further away from understanding exactly who I was, what I wanted, and where I was going.

Before going off to college, I sought advice because I was unsure. Not only was college a new experience, it was one I would have to face on my own. I realized after my first semester that nothing and no one could have prepared me for my own, individual experience. So, to offer my own advice at this point would seem contradictory and even short-sighted, seeing as though I've only been at school for a semester. But I will offer it anyway.

Going to college is not about going to school, it is about going away. No matter how far you go, or how close you stay to home, college is the first step you take away from childhood and into adulthood. I was supported financially by my parents and I could call home anytime I wanted, but I had to cope with my new surroundings on my own. The first few months of school were amazing and dismal. I was having fun and doing well, keeping to a schedule, and making the best of my opportunities. On the other hand, my relationships from high school were disintegrating and it saddened me to see friends drift further away from me. I stood by as my girlfriend slowly became just a friend and as my good friends that I had seen everyday at school became voices over the phone or words in a letter. For me, it was difficult to juggle the new and the old, to come to terms with where I used to be and where I was going. Yes, the work is harder, there are people to meet, more freedoms, more distractions, et cetera. But the hardest part about college for me was that it meant losing part of my life back home.

Here I sit, typing away at my computer, hours before the deadline of this book (I've been pushing it for quite some time now) and my winter break is two weeks gone. I have six more days at home and I am starting to come to the realization that I have a lot of work to do when I go back. There's all the schoolwork I'll be busy with, and there's the tricky situation about rearranging my schedule so I can get to the gym six days a week. I want to figure who my true friends are and who will start to appear at my side less and less. I want to date this girl I've liked for the whole first semester and I intensely want to become a better writer. Vacation has been relaxing. I've reconnected with some friends and lost touch with others. I've found that the beach and the ocean are just as I left them (if maybe a little colder) and I can see that I am different than I was when I set out for school in August. There was a moment not too long ago when I realized that the place I grew up in was no longer my home. And though I felt comfortable and secure, loved and protected, I was still searching for something else. The current is pulling me blindly through a foggy ocean, along through deep waters, deeper than any I have ever been in before. There was a time when I would panic and fight to find my way back to shore, back to where the sun was shining and the gulls were laughing, but now I simply choose to relax and let my body drift along to wherever the current wants to take me. For now, that is back to New Orleans and an unknowable set of new experiences.

—Doug Barry, Tulane University,
December 2004

Index